Prodigal in the Parsonage

*Encouragement for Ministry Leaders
Whose Child Rejects Faith*

Judi Braddy

Beacon Hill Press of Kansas City
Kansas City, Missouri

ISBN 083-412-2065

Printed in the
United States of America

Cover Design: Paul Franitza

Library of Congress Cataloging-in-Publication Data

Braddy, Judi, 1948-
  Prodigal in the parsonage : encouragement for ministry leaders whose child rejects faith / Judi Braddy.
    p. cm.
  Includes bibliographical references.
  ISBN 0-8341-2206-5 (pbk.)
  1. Children of clergy—Religious life. 2. Parenting—Religious aspects—Christianity. 3. Clergy—Family relationships. I. Title.

  BV4396.B73 2004
  253'.22—dc22

                                                    2004020291

10 9 8 7 6 5 4 3 2 1

To Forrest Damon, Derek Ian, and Dustin James

Whether two steps forward or three steps back,
it's never more than one step home.

And to Jim
Friend, husband, dad, grampa, and pastor.
You're simply the best.

Contents

Acknowledgments

No book is ever the work of just one person. The following thanks are in order.

To the many in ministry who were willing to be transparent and share with me their own journeys down the prodigal path. Though I was not able to fit all your stories into the book, what an encouragement to hear your often painful—but always hopeful and insightful—stories!

To those who prayed and encouraged me through the literary process. Your timing was always divinely directed.

To Bonnie Perry for believing, without really knowing, that I could write this book. Thanks also to Judi Perry, editor extraordinaire, along with all those at Beacon Hill Press who have made being a first-time book author a joy.

To my cheering section at Sacramento Christian Writers, thanks for five years of support and encouragement. I wouldn't be where I am without you.

To my close writing buddies, Jan Coleman and Laura Jensen Walker, for your persistent prodding which often came in the form of a good kick in the creative process under the guise of a proper English tea.

To my dogs, Freckles and Peanut, who curled companionably by the computer, no matter what hour inspiration or insomnia came to call. Such quiet comfort—even with the snores and snuffles!

To my three sons, who gave me permission to poke at some very painful places. Whatever happens with the book, guys, I believe that what we have all learned in the prodigal process will pay eternal royalties.

To my husband, Jim, who traveled solo for four months so I could stay home and write about a few of the rough roads we've already traveled together.

To God be the glory for the things He has done, and continues to do, in all our lives.

Introduction

*In his heart a man plans his course, but the
Lord determines his steps.*
—Prov. 16:9

It was a good plan. I had come to my fourth year at the Mount
Hermon (California) Christian Writer's Conference—where the
crème de la crème of editors, agents, and authors congregate for a
fast-paced week of learning and networking—armed with a proposal
for a devotional. It seemed reasonable. After all, everything I'd previously published pointed to "I" for inspiration on the contribution
compass.

Problem was, I'd forgotten my favorite alteration of an old
adage: "God works in mischievous ways, His wonders to perform."

Even as I plotted my own way down the publishing path, God
was devising a divine detour. Three days into the conference, I
found myself slipping into the empty seat at the dinner table next
to Bonnie Perry from Beacon Hill Press of Kansas City.

Not far into the meal, Bonnie and I began to dialogue about a
writing project already in process dealing with prodigal children.
As a pastor's wife with hands-on experience, I'd been asked to
contribute a few thoughts and anecdotes. "You know, Bonnie," I
mused, "I've always thought someone should write a book specifically for ministry families called 'Prodigal in the Parsonage.'"

Fork poised in midair, she leaned toward me. "Do you know
someone who could write that book?"

"Well, yes—I could." *Wait a minute,* I thought. *What am I saying? I do short inspiration and humor. Besides, I have a dynamite
devotional idea.*

"If you can have a proposal to me in six weeks, I'll consider
contracting that book."

Gulp.

Even as I heard myself saying, "Sure, I can do that," I began to
wonder.

Can I, Lord? Thirty-seven years in ministry, nineteen of it on the prodigal path, provided me plenty of material. And hadn't my husband, Jim, and I conducted numerous seminars for ministry families dealing with prodigal children? We'd candidly and willingly shared our journey to infuse hope in others.

But writing a book is a different thing. Did I really want our pain recorded in permanent ink? Besides, a successful story requires a happy ending, right?

Our personal prodigal parable was still in the editing process.

When dinner concluded, I hurried to call Jim. If anyone could put this in perspective, it was my practical husband. Surely, he'd have reservations.

"So," I said after blurting out all the details, "are we ready to do this?"

"Honey, if the Lord has opened this door, I think you should walk through it and see what happens."

Of all the times for him to be supportive!

The next day, in Mount Hermon's rustic but majestic redwood sanctuary, I sat silently enjoying the marvelous music. As waves of worship washed over me, tears began to fall. *Lord, I want to write a book out of my joy, not out of my pain.*

My real dilemma had finally bubbled to the surface.

The thought that followed could have come only from God. *You never write only out of joy or pain. It is pain that gives your writing depth; it is joy that gives your writing hope.*

Isn't the same true of life and ministry as well?

Suddenly I knew. The book I would write needed to be one assuring us that even when God chooses to use our own children to teach us some painful lessons, He has a plan and purpose. Even as we're struggling to make sense of our circumstances and their effect on ministry, He can still use both our pain and joy to encourage others.

What about our boys? I wondered. *Would they be comfortable with the idea of a tell-all from Mom?* If not, my heart told me there would be no pursuing it. When I finally spoke to my sons, I assured them my plan was not to drag out all our dirty laundry—only to use the torn pieces of our family quilt as a comforter to pass on to others.

Without hesitation, each one echoed the same thing: "Go for it, Mom."

Someone recently asked me, "How can that be? They're still struggling with spiritual issues." True, there are chapters of our personal story yet to be written, but thank God, we've moved beyond the rough draft stage. My prayer from the beginning has been that as God uses this book to encourage others, He will allow it to be a healing tool for our own family.

So with my kids' permission and my husband's encouragement, I set about to fulfill the assignment. It began with an E-mail appeal to others in ministry, those willing to share their own painful and poignant prodigal reflections, to find out how they navigated their way through similar situations.

As the stories poured in, it confirmed not only the number of ministry families dealing with prodigal children but also the need for this kind of book. It's evident that the enemy is increasingly targeting us, so much that I was prompted to add a chapter on spiritual warfare.

I even found myself dug deep in the trenches as I labored over the manuscript—from a plague of ticks (I kid you not) to an infected thumb, not to mention the emotional journey of reliving some painful memories.

The result is a book of encouragement, with hope and a hint of humor woven into every chapter. There are no attempts to provide all the answers. The many unseen and varying circumstances make that impossible. And no formulas. I didn't have that kind of information or expertise. Besides, my experience has been that formulas don't come with guarantees.

Rather, the book has a two-fold purpose: to share practical perspectives on how the challenges of having a prodigal child can affect ministry issues; but more so, the ways our lives, families, and ministries can be enriched if we stay the course and apply the lessons.

My husband, Jim, and I pray that the journey we share will provide insight and aid for ministry families chosen by God to love a prodigal in the parsonage.

1

Where Does a Pastor Go to Resign?

*Be on your guard; stand firm in the faith;
be men of courage, be strong.*
—1 Cor. 16:13

Autumn leaves of red, gold, and bronze scattered the pathway like giant, intricately shaped confetti. My husband walked beside me, hands in his pants pockets, gazing ahead. As I dangled my arm loosely through his, late afternoon sunlight cast lengthy shadows behind us. It was a perfect day, except for the troubled frown that cast its own shadow across Jim's handsome features. "I'm going to resign the church," he said evenly.

Something deep in my heart crunched like a dry leaf.

It had been an unusually vibrant season in northern California, a nostalgic reminder of our growing-up years in the Midwest. We met in the fall and courted as he finished college, preparing to enter the ministry. In those days, our hand-in-hand walks across campus overflowed with casual conversation, warmed by laughter, love, and eager expectation. Now almost 20 autumns later, the frosty resolve in his voice chilled the air around us.

It certainly would not be the first time we had left one church to shepherd another. But the circumstances this time were very different. We had been in this church of 150 people less than two years and were really just settling in. Jim had developed close ties with staff, and I was teaching a women's Bible study and participating in other ministries. We loved it here. From the morning we first walked through the sanctuary doors, it felt like home. The congregation embraced us like extended family and responded warmly to my husband's contemporary, down-to-earth style of ministry. They caught his enthusiasm for finding new and creative ways to reach the surrounding community. By the end of the first year, we were holding two Sunday morning services and making plans to expand our facilities. God had directed us to this place for this time. We knew it without a doubt.

Then family problems took us on an unexpected journey with many devastating twists and turns.

Stopping on the path, I looked away, fixing my eyes on a branch with one clinging leaf. Somehow I identified. "Honey, we already talked about this. I thought we were in agreement that resigning is not the answer."

"Then what is?" He stared down the winding path, as if the answer might appear at the end.

"I don't know. Surely the church won't hold us responsible for our children's actions."

"Maybe not, Judi. But I just can't continue to stand behind the pulpit and preach to others when I don't even know how to help my own family."

I looked at a face that was sad but determined—a determination I knew well. He had made up his mind.

Following the move to this pastorate, it had been only six months before the difficulties began to surface. Our three handsome and energetic sons were ages 8, 11, and 13. Outgoing and seemingly well adjusted, they had already made numerous moves—often inherent with ministry—quite easily. This time, though, they were forced to leave the Christian school they liked. For three years they had thrived there academically and been involved in a myriad of sports and extracurricular activities. All their friends were part of the church or school. It was a happy and protected environment.

Then the call came from Sacramento to pastor a new church— a smaller church. My ambitious, innovative husband was intrigued by the challenge of applying his gifts to helping it grow. Its obvious potential presented an irresistible opportunity. Unfortunately, it also presented a cut in salary and benefits, which meant tuition for Christian school was out of the question. Our boys would have to return to public school. Homeschooling was relatively new and uncharted at the time, so we never considered it as an option. For our two elementary age boys, it wasn't such a drastic change. But our oldest son, who had just turned 13 and had entered the eighth grade, was thrust into adolescent crisis.

Now he was just another kid in a big school trying to find his place. Where did he belong? He tried getting involved through sports, but they were much more competitive. Never one to just sit on the bench, he soon gave up. When you've been a big frog in a little pond, it's tough to feel like a tadpole again.

Unfortunately, the youth group in our small church didn't offer much for his age in the way of companionship or excitement. So he gravitated toward those at school who most readily accepted him—others who didn't flow in the mainstream either. They weren't necessarily bad kids, but kids who offered no spiritual support, no reinforcement that his values were worth keeping. The more we tried to keep him close and involved in the church, the less he showed interest. Being included, being part of the crowd, was what mattered most. He wanted to hang out with his school friends. Yet even with them, he was lonely and hurting as he struggled between compromise and conscience.

As the months passed, we watched him grow angrier, pain etched in the hardness of his face. Soon he was begging us, "Please let me go back to the other school. I can live with my friend, John. His mom said it's OK."

Break up our family? We couldn't consider it. We were a ministry family, after all. We would continue to trust God, and everything would be fine. Surely this was a passing phase. He adjusted before; he would eventually adjust again.

He didn't.

The months ahead found us trudging into frightening and unfamiliar territory as our son's anger and frustration turned inward. Soon our entire family was involved in his struggles. The other boys had their own adjustments and were watching to see how we would handle this new behavior at home. We wondered, too. Over the next few months we tried every positive reinforcement ploy: verbal affirmation, compromises, deals, even monetary rewards for good behavior. We talked, we prayed, and we preached. Little good that did. *Maybe it's just temporary,* we told ourselves. *Let's hold our ground until things smooth out.* But as every boundary we set was willfully crossed, it felt as if we were being backed into a minefield of tension-filled emotion. Take the wrong step, and something was going to blow.

We didn't know how to help our son. By this time he was regularly breaking curfew, smoking, lying to us about his activities, and performing poorly in school both academically and socially. We also suspected he was experimenting with drugs and alcohol. He showed little remorse when we confronted him and was belligerent toward our attempts to discipline him. After these confrontations, it was not unusual for him to storm out of the house. Sometimes it took a day or two for us to track him down. Desperate, we tried a number of counselors and intervention programs, with limited success. To make matters worse, our middle son was beginning to reflect some of the same behavioral problems. As the situation spiraled out of control, we hung onto faith, prayed for wisdom, and labored to console each other.

And our problems were quickly becoming apparent to our church.

Is there anything more devastating for a minister than setting out to win the world but then losing a grip on his own family? What a paradox! Here he is, the spiritual quarterback, running the ball into the end zone for the Lord while his kids are tearing down the goal posts and burning them in protest before the crowd. While it might seem reasonable for fledglings in the faith to make a wrong play here or there, the pastor is the one who comes up with strategies and calls the spiritual shots. At the first sign of trouble, the obvious question is *How can this possibly be happening? We've tried to do everything right. We followed all the rules. Where did we go wrong?* Questions become silent specters that haunt our thoughts and prayers. More frightening is to hear them echoing around the pews. I vividly remember the Sunday morning someone approached to tell me she had heard about my son getting in a fight and to assure me of her prayers. It was the first I knew about it—not quite the way I wanted to find out.

You would think in our socially enlightened age, people wouldn't still be putting ministers' families on pedestals— especially after the prominently televised falls from grace of a few bigtime evangelists. On the contrary, these only served to heighten people's awareness, inside and outside the pews, of what is evangelically expected. So while the local minister's misdeeds may not make the national news, they still often headline the hometown hotline. Faster than you can say *Google-dot-com,* words that used to cackle over clotheslines crackle over E-mail.

As soon as the preacher blows it, everybody knows it.

Seems the congregation still has expectations: not only will the minister practice what he preaches, but his family will too. His home should be the model manse for their spiritual subdivision, complete with glass walls. Whatever happens there, the pastor's high visibility provides the equivalent of a PowerPoint presentation bullet-marking his faults and failures—on a 46" screen.

When he experiences family problems, a distinct line is quickly drawn between him and the average parishioner's family.

Unfair? Maybe. Yet no one understands this better and expects it more than the pastor himself. Like it or not, it goes with the territory. So he and the Mrs. do their best to ensure their cherubs toe the line. When things happen to the contrary, the feelings of frustration, failure, and humiliation are magnified. No wonder when caught between church and family, many see resignation as the only honorable, face-saving way out. There's just one small problem.

Where does a pastor go to resign?

Certainly you can hand the church board a piece of official stationery with the typed words indicating your intentions. Following a clearing of throats and mumbled objections, they may even accept it. But the reality is that though the board invited you to this particular place of ministry, they did not issue your divine commission. That came from God, whose "gifts and . . . call are irrevocable" (Rom. 11:25). You may leave the church, but you don't just walk away from the call of a lifetime.

On that long-ago autumn day, no one understood that dilemma better than Jim and me. Struggling at times with an overwhelming sense of frustration and failure as parents, our walks had become temporary escapes from the stress. Maybe we hoped a change of scenery might reveal what had gone wrong and how to fix it, all the while knowing we couldn't go back or change the present circumstances. All we could do was pray for future wisdom. Was there a possibility of continued ministry in the middle of what seemed like such a mess? Maybe we shouldn't even continue to try.

First and foremost, of course, we were concerned for our children. But Jim's concern was compounded as he contemplated how our situation might reflect negatively on the church. His was a three-fold obligation—to his family, to the church, and to God. I worried, knowing that on a crucial, personal level he was questioning his effectiveness on all counts. In the end, it was my husband's strong sense of personal integrity that prevailed over all other considerations.

Two days later he presented his resignation to the church board.

I've wondered many times since that fall day in 1985 where we would be now had it not been for six incredible, godly men who tore up that piece of official stationery with the typed words indicating my husband's intentions. Instead, they stood that morning encircling him in prayer. One board member spoke clearly: "Pastor, do you think we haven't been through this with some of our own kids? No way will we let you walk through this alone." In that awesome atmosphere they committed themselves to standing with us and supporting our ministry. Because of their leading, the entire church followed suit through our seven-year tenure of ministry. We're eternally grateful, especially after hearing of other pastors who have been less fortunate.

That day was a true crossroads in more ways than we could know. But God knew. As circumstances unfolded, we would desperately need that affirmation and support. Even today we find strength in the memory. By God's grace our ministry flourished, but the struggles at home were just beginning. That changing season of the year ushered in a time of change in our lives, one that would last for many seasons to come.

What does a pastor do when it becomes apparent that problems in the parsonage aren't going away? Is resigning your church the only answer when your home is in turmoil? There are too many variables for a one-size-fits-all answer. We've seen many ministers over the years give up too soon and lose not just their churches but future ministry, family, and in some extreme cases, their relationships with the Lord. That should never happen.

Dear friend in ministry, God has called you for a purpose. Never doubt it for a moment. He's ready to walk with you through these difficult days. No matter how things seem, He loves you, and He loves your children—even more than you do. "The one who calls you is faithful and he will do it," Scripture says (1 Thess. 5:24). Do what? Keep us blameless until the coming of our Lord Jesus Christ (see v. 23). Now I ask you—if God sees us as blameless, why are we often so hard on ourselves?

Could it be we suffer from a bit of spiritual pride? As ministers, we know God's word. We teach it. We practice it. We depend on His faithfulness to it. Then one day God asks us to put our faith where our family is, and suddenly we're floundering. Why? Because, contrary to congregational concepts and our own doctrine-induced delusions, we don't really walk on water. We give swimming lessons. So when we find ourselves in the deep end, what happens? We automatically kick into preacher mode and start applying the correct strokes—until we realize it's farther to the side of the pool than we anticipated.

Then, like any panicked parishioner, we throw all pride and pretensions aside and resort to doing the really spiritual thing: we dog paddle like crazy. Too late. Weak and weary, going down for the third time, we hear ourselves speak those incredible, scriptural words of faith: *Lord, don't you care that I'm drowning here? Maybe I should just take a big gulp and get it over with.*

It's resignation time.

My husband had an experience a number of years ago that he often uses as a sermon illustration. He had taken a group from one of our churches on a missionary outreach to the Philippines. After a strenuous week of services to the church and community, they were treated to a much-needed day of rest and relaxation. This involved sailing in an outrigger canoe to a small, nearby island. Heading out, the midmorning sun turned each wave into a translucent blue-green prism. The sky was a cloudless cerulean canopy. The group spent a glorious day snorkeling, beach combing, and enjoying a picnic.

As they climbed into the outrigger for the return trip, Jim noticed some foreboding clouds in the distance. A stiff wind chopped the sea's surface into frothy white caps. Not even halfway back, a sudden storm had the group riding six-to-eight-foot waves. As water broke over the outrigger's hull, my husband remembers becoming distinctly aware of two things. The shore was still a long way off, and the captain was the only one with a life jacket. Jim knew he could never swim that far, so he did the only logical thing—he stayed in the boat.

The trip seemed to take forever, because instead of making straight for shore, the captain kept turning the outrigger to ride up one side of a wave, then down the other. Otherwise the boat would capsize, and they would all be tossed into that angry ocean. Time stood still. With a death grip on the sides of the boat, Jim ventured a look at the captain. His face was set but serene. It was apparent that he knew exactly what he was doing.

Eventually, with much thanksgiving, they made it to shore.

The lessons Jim relates from that experience are these: storms come quickly and when we least expect them. It may take longer to ride out the waves than we anticipated. When that happens, there are only two things to do—(1) stay in the boat, and (2) trust the captain.

Many who've had a near-drowning experience will tell you they see their whole lives flash before them in those last moments. I'm sure this is both frightening and enlightening. It's frightening because the unedited video of our lives can be quite revealing. It's enlightening because it forces us to face life honestly with re-newed priorities.

Have you ever had a spiritual "splash-back?" I have. Maybe you'll relate to these.

My first splash-back: strive as we might, we weren't the perfect parents. I'm sure all of us started with the goal to be as good as or better at raising kids than our parents were. We memorized the child-rearing books, attended parenting seminars, joined the Point-ers for Parents Sunday School class, and clipped out helpful articles.

Still our greatest parenting example is God himself. He loves His children, and His greatest desire is that they be in fellowship with Him. So what did *He* do? Like any good parent, right from the get-go, He provided Adam and Eve with a flawless living environ-ment in the Garden of Eden. A place to walk, talk, have picnics—you know the story. He also set boundaries, which He lovingly monitored. Even with everything going for them, it didn't take long for the kids to tumble into trouble. Sound familiar? Not unlike many preachers' kids, it boiled down to an identity problem that resulted in rebellion and some pretty severe consequences. Of course, they also had some unsolicited support from a certain snake.

From Genesis on, God's Word illustrates clearly why there is an unavoidable probability of prodigals. As long as there is temptation and free will, there will be those who choose to believe a lie rather than embrace God's perfect plan for their lives. They see God's laws only as an attempt to prevent them from living their own way, and they rebel. Consequently, God has a plethora of prodigal children wandering the world today. And we think *we* have problems! The eternal Good News is that God has another plan already in place. Here's our hope. Even when our best-laid plans fail, He still has a plan for our prodigals.

My second splash-back: we are not the only shepherds struggling with a straying sheep. It's possible that no home comes under tougher attack by the enemy than that of ministry families. Just as Satan infiltrated God's perfect garden, he's still attempting to devour many preachers' pastures. He would really like us to just pack up and move on. I don't know about you, but it makes me mad enough to dig in my heels and stay. I'm not leaving until my lambs find the way home. Just thinking about it makes me want to punch the devil in the nose—which I have many times, spiritually speaking. We must not give him the satisfaction of our resignation. Ministry may carry a higher risk of enemy attack, but that's because we're doing something right. It's a divine calling—remember?

It's also a very personal one.

My third splash-back: While we chose at some point to answer God's call to ministry, our children didn't. They were born into a pastor's home whether they wanted to be or not. It's not unusual for preachers' kids to go through a questioning time, even a rebelling phase. That's not necessarily bad. In fact, it can be an important part of their spiritual growth. It means they're sorting things out and making a personal decision about serving God, not just riding on their parents' spiritual coattails.

It could even be that God is asking some of them to try on the clerical collar or missionary mantle for size. Maybe it scares them to death. After all, they know firsthand what this ministry gig is all about. They've seen their parents struggle to make ends meet on a pastor's meager salary. They've watched Dad drag in after a tough board meeting or midnight hospital call. They've heard him being raked over the coals by an irate parishioner. Yes, they know firsthand about the demands placed on the pastor's time, not to mention the expectations for his wife and family. They may be thinking, *No way.* The pressure on pastors' kids to perform is incredible. No wonder they need time to figure out whether it's God speaking or Memorex.

Don't throw in the mantle just because your kids are asking some tough questions.

It is true that some kids' simple struggles develop into dynamic dilemmas. Why is that? I wish I knew. There are too many contributing factors to come up with any one formula: personalities, family dynamics, hurtful situations, unforeseen crisis, outside influences, to name just a few. Only God knows every individual heart, hurt, and circumstance.

In either case, the decisions our children make are ultimately between them and God. If only we could manage not to take them so personally. When ministry is your life, the feeling of personal rejection has so many added dimensions.

Here's a concluding splash of truth. Though resigning may remove you from the immediate pressures and embarrassment of your situation, it does not necessarily eliminate the problem. In most cases our lives are only complicated by a whole new cycle of guilt and frustration. And did I mention failure? The last thing we need when our children are facing an identity crisis is one of our own. The assurance that we remain in the center of God's will goes a long way toward helping us cope when everything else seems to be crashing down around us.

Despite the personal pain, Jim and I stayed the course in ministry, and it has rewarded us on many levels. It has not been easy. But as we've fought Satan for possession and sought God for wisdom, our prayer muscles have been strengthened, and we've had to keep our Sword sharpened. Our situation has also opened doors of ministry that have allowed us to touch hearts and lives in ways and places we never imagined, not to mention those who have touched us. More often than not, at the end of services conducted to encourage others, we find ourselves enveloped in empathetic prayer. Or people will come to share a personal story of victory. A number of these encouraging stories will be woven as illustrations through other chapters in this book.

The words of love and encouragement spoken into our lives over the years are too many to number. Whether they come verbally or in the form of frequent E-mails, occasional letters, or annual Christmas greetings, they're always timely. Just recently a memorial service held at the church where our prodigal journey began brought together many of the original parishioners. My heart was touched by those who, after all these years, made a point to ask about our children.

One thing is certain. Without the mooring of ministry and faithfulness of friends, the journey would have been longer and lonelier.

Even so, one of the biggest hurdles for my husband was talking with other ministers regarding this very sensitive part of our lives. Doesn't it seem like this would be the one place a pastor could let down appearances? Not necessarily. As ministers, we all strive foremost for God's approval, but running a close second is respect among our own peers. We tend to guard our reputations like the head usher counting Sunday morning's offering.

That's understandable.

We may not like to acknowledge it, but ministers can be a bit competitive with a tendency toward comparison. Strong opinions about what will make or break your ministry have been known to flow freely in seminarian circles. There is also a fair amount of critical thinking. Sad to say, some ministers are quick to make assumptions about where you are and how you got there. I know, because we've done it ourselves and had to ask forgiveness. More than once we've made harsh judgments or negative comments about fellow ministers without taking time to gather facts or hear both sides of the story. When you suddenly find yourself in need of grace, those wincing memories make a hearty filling for humble pie. No wonder a pastor with a kid kicking in the closet would feel a bit threatened. Just the thought of being that vulnerable could subject us to the recurring nightmare of standing behind a glass pulpit wearing nothing but a Bible and boxers.

For my husband it was not so much a pride issue as a privacy issue. He's just not the type of personality who's inclined to share personal problems of any kind—especially those concerning family. While I respect and appreciate that, I was concerned that he had no confidant who understood the pressures of ministry. I could call a number of close friends for prayer and support, but my husband didn't seem to feel that freedom or need. This was the subject of more than one "There must be other pastors going through this besides us" discussions.

Then a few years down the prodigal path, one of our denominational officials phoned.

"Jim, I'm hoping you might be willing to conduct a workshop

at our upcoming leadership conference."

"Sure. What did you have in mind?"

"I'd like you to share a testimony on the topic of prodigals in the parsonage."

"Oh."

Though a number of close ministry friends knew the specifics of our struggle, this was Jim's first invitation to address a formal group. It was also his first inkling that our situation must have reached executive ears.

We discussed it later that evening over coffee. "I don't imagine there'll be a large number interested in hearing about this." He was trying to convince himself.

"Probably not," I agreed and encouraged him to do it. "I'm sure it will be helpful to those who do come. Anyway, you sure have a mountain of material." He agreed to accept the challenge.

When he walked into the conference room that day, armed but apprehensive about sharing our story, he was nothing short of shocked. The room was packed. Could there really be that many ministry friends struggling with prodigal issues? He soon found out. Not only were they dealing with the common emotions we share when our children stray from faith, but they were also struggling with the devastating ripple effect on their ministries.

My husband also discovered that many had suffered silently for a long time. Somehow that gave him the resolve to be open and honest. He spoke not only about the feelings of disgrace at the black mark on our ministry but also about dashed hopes for our son and fears for his future. As Jim risked being transparent, those pastors found the courage and a safe forum to share their own painful prodigal stories.

"My daughter is living with an abusive boyfriend."

"My son's been through drug rehab three times now."

"We don't even know where our child is."

"We never get to see our grandkids."

"I thought we were the only ones."

"We've felt so ashamed and guilty."

Many tears of release, healing, and hope were shed that day as we prayed and encouraged one another.

One of my favorite examples appears in a Psalm written by a fellow shepherd. David was soon to understand the pain of his own prodigal son big time when he wrote, "You have taken account of my wanderings; Put my tears in Your bottle. Are they not in Your book?" (Ps. 56:8, NASB). Picture that. Somewhere in heaven, God is collecting our tears, similar to the way we keep all our children's report cards and baby teeth, perhaps. I've imagined Him on some eternal afternoon taking out a big, tattered box with my name on it and saying, "Look here, Judi. You had quite a journey with those boys. It appears you took a few detours here and there, but the important thing is you stayed the course. Well done."

And our tears? I suppose, like baby teeth, they're necessary only for a season, since Scripture tells us that in heaven there will be no more crying. Still, for now, it's nice to know He's keeping track.

After that eye-opening conference, Jim and I agreed on a very different type of resignation. If this was our path, short or long, we would find ways to encourage fellow pastors and others in the same situation. Together with them, we would believe that in the pain of our prodigals God has both a personal and far-reaching purpose.

Most important, we resigned our situation to God, trusting Him for strength and wisdom to keep following His direction, not only for ministry but for everything.

Since that first workshop, Jim and I have both had countless opportunities to share our experience and message of encouragement in many public venues. And over the years we've been invited to a lot of homecoming parties. "Our son is back home," one minister tearfully announced to us at a recent retreat. "I wanted you to be the first besides family to know." Their son had been away from home for many months and had ended up in jail. It was there where he called his parents to tell them that he was scared and tired of running. He wanted help finding his way back to God and family. A few weeks later, they threw a welcome-home party straight out of Scripture. The menu featured grilled chicken instead of fatted calf, but it was a celebration that family will never forget. What a joy and encouragement when someone we've cried and prayed with shares a prodigal praise report!

Where are you in the prodigal process today? Do your kids simply need an open ear and some honest answers? Maybe some are truly testing the boundaries, drawing lines in the sand to protest expectations and flaunt their freedom. Perhaps they've already slipped from the safety of the sheepfold, slamming the gate behind them. You can only stand frozen, fighting the urge to chase after them. Your child may be deep in that dreaded distant land, running in vain from God.

That became the ongoing heartache we eventually had to face.

Over many years we squinted daily for that speck on the horizon, for our son's familiar stride on that distant road. We've lived through situations and resulting circumstances that were a pastor's worst nightmare. Even today, two of our grown sons are at arm's length from the faith we tried to instill. Though we no longer feel compelled to rescue them, and though we try hard to resist tossing out unsolicited advice, it's interesting how often they ask for it. They're inching closer, and we are praying harder than ever. And we've never stopped hanging out the lantern of love.

The one thing we must never resign is hope.

Whatever the circumstances, my heartfelt prayer is that your precious prodigals won't be far down the road before coming to their senses and hot-footing it back toward home. I encourage you—don't move from your stand or forsake your ministry. When it's time for your prodigal to return, you need to be home. Trust God, and keep the porch light burning.

Lord, some who are reading these words today have their resignations written. Wrap Your loving arms around them just now. Comfort them as only a loving Father can do. Encourage them through Your written Word and Your whispered peace. Confirm once more Your call upon their lives and ministries. Give them courage to continue, strength to hold tight, and faith to keep believing. Assure them that they're not alone and that neither are their children. In the name of Your own precious Son, Jesus Christ, the Great Shepherd, who still seeks to save the lost. Amen.

We all have days when we're full of hope and other days when we struggle with a myriad of overwhelming emotions. The following chapters address both. Together we'll explore the issues related to prodigals that affect ministry, sharing many different stories of hope and help. This book is for those of you in ministry who are waiting, watching, and praying for a child who is missing and missed. May it provide comfort in the waiting, especially in those sleepless hours, give you company in the vigil, and nurture hope for the coming celebration.

And if you're still not sure how it all happened in the first place or what's in the forecast for the future, take heart. Heaven knows, and that's enough.

2

What in Heaven's Name Has Happened?

*In my anguish I cried to the LORD,
and he answered by setting me free.*
—Ps. 118:5

We had just slogged through a second wet winter in our new church and home. The Christmas holidays provided a seasonal reprieve from the previous autumn's angst. So far we had managed to jump the puddles of potential problems into spring. With no recent splashes, hope seemed to grow with each tender green sprout. Then one morning around 2 A.M., I awoke abruptly and sat up in bed, listening. Parental instinct had shaken me from a deep sleep. Something was wrong.

As my feet touched the bare wooden floor, an icy current shivered through my body. Was it just the early-spring chill or something more? Walking apprehensively down the hall to the boys' shared bedroom, I flipped on the light. Our oldest son's bed was empty.

Dear Jesus, I said, and then called to my husband.

It didn't take long to search the house, only to discover the sliding patio door unlocked. He was definitely gone. But where? With whom? He had never in his 14 years done this before. As I prayed and worried, in no rational order, my husband made a drive through the neighborhood. The look on his face when he returned told me. Nothing. There was nothing to do but sit out the wee hours, weighing our options. It appeared he had left on his own accord, but how long should we wait? *If he's not back in time for school,* we decided, *we'll call the police.* Sleep was a lost cause.

When our son attempted to sneak back in just before dawn, his first reaction to seeing us was surprise. Then defiance. Despite our incredible relief that he was safe, the inevitable angry confrontation followed.

"Where have you been? Don't you know we were worried sick? What if something had happened? We wouldn't even know where to look for you!"

He hadn't expected to be caught, so his best defense was a good offense. Shrugging off our concern, he showed little remorse and even less intent to explain his actions. Faced with a stubborn standoff, our anger melted into tearful weariness. Then the ultimate question: "Why in heaven's name are you doing this?"

That's when he fell sadly silent. He had no idea. And neither did we. Nor did we have a clue that behavioral patterns were forming that would result in many sleepless nights to come.

If someone had told me when my boys were small that someday they would walk away from their Christian faith, I would not have believed it. They were virtually born in church—one labor even began as I was playing the piano for worship. When they were babies we dedicated them to the Lord. When they were children they attended Sunday School, Vacation Bible School, and church camp. They memorized scripture and played lead roles in musicals. Those were days of happy involvement. Through their beginning adolescent years we monitored their friends and activities, applied spiritual guidance and discipline. At home we read Bible stories and then prayed God's blessing and protection as we tucked them into bed.

One of our funniest memories combines two of those points. When our middle son was about four years old, he got into trouble one day for making a mess. I sent him to his room, promising that he would get a spanking after I cleaned it up. Distracted by a phone call, I finally found him napping like an angel. Of course, I lost my resolve. That night, straightening his room before bedtime, I opened the closet. There in a pile lay every pair of undies he owned. He had put them all on in anticipation of the spanking, then taken them off when he knew the coast was clear.

A funny story, it also illustrates an early ingenuity to avoid the consequences of his actions, something he developed into a fine art later on.

Maybe we didn't always manage to be consistent or discipline fairly, but we must have done something right. We've loved our children and, above all, wanted them to find happiness and reach their full potential serving God. At some point all three of our boys made confessions of faith and were baptized. I know our story parallels that of most ministry families.

So what on earth happened? It's the question every parent of a prodigal asks.

Now imagine you're halfway around the world asking that question. Our friends Mike and Lynne Chandler were one of few missionary couples living in Mzuzu, an isolated city in northern Malawi, when they received a call from their son, Paul. At the time Paul was living in California near his married sister, Michelle, attending college. His parents' joy at hearing their son's voice soon turned to painful confusion.

"I'm just calling to tell you I've stopped attending church and meeting with my campus Christian fellowship group." His words echoed across the delay on the international phone connection. Before Mike or Lynne could formulate a response, Paul proceeded.

"I've only been going to please Michelle, anyway. I still believe in God, but I'm just not that interested in spiritual things anymore. There's no reason for me to keep attending." Then a weak apology: "I thought I should be honest with you."

Lynne tumbled into an initial myriad of emotions—surprise, shock, and fear—but tried hard not to let them register in her voice. When you're that far away, you certainly want to keep the lines of communication open. Mike states it simply. "We felt so helpless." It wasn't until after they hung up that hurt and anger surfaced. "How did he get like this?" they asked each other. Then "How stupid can he be?"

In other words, what on earth had happened? More than they wanted to know. It would be a long three years separated by miles of mission field before they found out.

Like these and other dear ministry friends, I've prayed for divine insight and analyzed our own situation until my brain hurts. I've worn a rut (and often found myself in one) back-pedaling down the road to where the problem started, only to pump wearily back carrying the same basketful of questions. Have we all endured these years of pain just because we made our son leave a school he liked? Would he have made better future choices had we stayed? Or were there things already in play that we could never have predicted or anticipated?

My conclusion? Given all the various contributing factors,

there's no single, earthly answer. It's much more complicated than that. We're dealing with personalities, perceptions, and personal choices. For any one of us to assume all the guilt for what eventually unfolds is a greater burden than one is able to bear. We may eventually understand some of what has come into play; other factors only eternity will reveal. Truly, only heaven can know.

But that doesn't keep us from experiencing earthly emotion, does it?

One of the most difficult things we're called on to do as ministers is comfort those who are going through a life-threatening illness or the death of a loved one. So many times we've sat on the edge of a hospital bed or stood at the end of a coffin, searching for words of comfort and hope, knowing that nothing but prayer, love, and time will make a difference. Through this process, most of us have become familiar with the five stages of grief: denial, anger, guilt, depression, and acceptance.

Has it ever occurred to you that dealing with a prodigal child can run that same gamut of emotions? Just as with sickness or death, we're grieving a frightening change, a devastating separation, and very real loss—a loss of childhood innocence and family relationships, of hopes and dreams, both theirs and our own, and in some cases critical, formative years that can never be recovered. Then, over this raging emotional maelstrom, a haunting hiss is heard: "Physician, heal thyself." As ministers we should know how, but . . .

It's hard enough when a child leaves home under positive circumstances. Many parents duel the dreaded empty nest syndrome with stiff upper lips, knowing that it's part of the natural, necessary process. I remember waving our youngest son off on his cross-country drive to a Midwestern Bible college. Though we were so pleased to see him pursuing ministry after his own years of identity struggles, he left an empty room in our home and hearts. Besides that, he was driving my convertible! No wonder I was crying.

Still, it's one thing to fly the nest, quite another to fall out of it. No wonder our first defense is denial.

This can't be happening to us, we think. *This happens only to other people's children. Clueless people. Messed-up people. Hypocritical people. Not godly pastor-people. And if it does—well, just maybe they're not as godly as everyone thought.* Nope. We're not ready to go there.

So we snuggle deeper into our sanctimonious security blanket. Hasn't God given us principles in his Word to follow and promises to believe? And what about divine protection? We can quote those verses word for word. We also know that these principles and promises are there to be applied, indicating that we'll inevitably encounter a difficult situation at some point. But A plus B still equals C, right? You just plug in a principle, appropriate a promise or two, and voila! Problem solved.

If only.

I'm in no way implying that we can't depend on God's principles and promises. Nor am I saying we shouldn't apply and appropriate them. They're our hope and our comfort, as well as what we comfort others with—ancient anchors, reliable refuges.

But not escape hatches.

When these times of testing come, we must understand and believe just as strongly in God's sovereignty, timing, and ultimate purposes. Otherwise faith can waver, and emotion can overwhelm us.

One of the verses well-meaning saints have routinely served me on a promise platter is Prov. 22:6—"Train a child in the way he should go, and when he is old he will not turn from it." As if it weren't already a staple in my devotional diet. If we train them, then they won't turn away. Seems like a foolproof formula. The part that's hard to digest is that little phrase "when he is old," indicating that we might have to wait a while—and wade through a lot. We don't want to do that. Like the guy who prayed for patience, we want results, and we want them *now*. We say, "Let's just get over this and get on with life," not for one minute wanting to consider that this might be life—ours, not someone else's.

Denial.

Still I love and appreciate those folks who speak softly and carry a big King James Version. I understand them. They want to be an encouragement, to provide an easy answer, a done deal. What they don't want is to think that a pastor could actually be losing a grip on his or her child. Why? If it can happen to a minister, it can happen to anyone. It can happen to them.

Now we come to the heart of the matter, not just for them but for us. We choose denial because we don't want to believe this could be happening. We don't want the pain, the humiliation, or the anxiety. Frankly, we don't want the hassle. It might interfere with our real ministry.

Maybe the hardest thing for us to accept as ministers is that we don't have immunity to problems. They affect us the same as others with one added dimension. Because we're expected to be an example, feelings of failure reach to the soles of our souls. Life is not a game of Monopoly. Nor do ministers have a monopoly on protection any more than perfection. When it finally dawns on us that we can't draw the get-out-of-jail-free card, we may switch to a new game: "Let's Make a Deal." We're now players on the bargaining board.

Lord, we say, *something has gone terribly wrong here. If You're trying to get my attention, You have it. Now just tell me what You want. More prayer? Fasting? A major attitude adjustment perhaps? I'll do whatever You say, I'll be whatever You want, if You'll just intervene.* Our hope is that by tweaking some personal impediment, we can tweak the circumstances. We'll do whatever it takes—unless, of course, it takes time. We have a ministry to run here, and people are beginning to ask questions. *Do something, Lord!*

You know it as well as I do. People bargain with God because they want a miracle. They want a miracle because they don't want to experience pain and its resulting emotions. Somehow as Christians we feel entitled to exemption. How much more for us who preach that miracles are still available and should be sought. We're talking not just personal disappointment but questionable credibility. *Is someone beginning to suspect there's a slow leak in the personal power connection?* No wonder that if circumstances don't immediately change, a new wave of emotions usually comes into play.

Anger, I've learned, is a natural reaction to three things: frustration, pain, and fear. Our initial frustration is obviously with our child. *What is he doing? Dumb kid. Doesn't he know how this is affecting us, how bad this is making us look?* In the bewildered words of our missionary friends, "How stupid can he be?"

For a long time I labored under the delusion that my sons just didn't get it. I had already decided this kind of behavior just wasn't acceptable and would not be allowed, and once they understood how much it was hurting them and us, they would stop. Despite my husband's concerned cautions, my brilliant plan of attack was to lecture more than I listened. I would just keep telling them over and over until the lightbulb came on.

Then one day the lightbulb *did* come on—mine. They knew what they were doing. And if it affected others adversely, that was the other person's problem. I was the one who didn't get it. When I did get it, I was mad.

It's hard not to be angry when we're hurt and frightened, hurt when the kids whose noses we've wiped don't seem to care enough to consider how we feel, frightened by wondering just how far this will go and what even the short-term consequences might be. How many people will it ultimately affect? What if something terrible happens to them while we're trying to get a handle on this? How could we ever live with the eternal worst-case scenario?

Kids by nature don't see the big picture. Being young, they don't have much experience to draw on. They simply live in the moment without much regard for the long-term consequences. Most of them—boys especially—just don't think the chances of anything bad happening are that great. In a Father's Day sermon celebrating the return of his own prodigal son, Pastor Jack Risner uses the illustration of a boy who climbs onto a roof to retrieve a lost ball. "Don't climb onto the roof," the boy is warned. "You may fall." His answer: "Yes, but I may not." Obviously many are willing to take that risk.

Others act out to express their own frustration, pain, and fear and to get our attention. And it works. The minute they act, we re-act. A lot of damage can be done in this initial stage of trying to patch our perfect parsonages. Free-flying frustration, like shrapnel, cuts deeply, leaving self-images scarred. Unless we're careful, words become grenades that blow up bridges. Prov. 29:22 says "An angry man stirs up dissension, and a hot-tempered one commits many sins." It seems anger can escalate into sin, even in a model manse.

When emotions simmer this close to the surface, they'll likely spill over on family and friends. Spouses disagree on the form and severity of discipline and then blame each other when it backfires. Siblings get caught in the crossfire. We respond defensively when well-meaning family members feel free to share unsolicited observations and advice. Even our closest, most caring friends can appear clueless to the divine dimensions of our dilemma.

Yet we need those who know us best to listen, pray, and encourage. They provide a perspective that we may have missed in the confusion and consternation. Family furnishes history while friends offer objectivity. Their outside insights are crucial to helping us keep a healthy perspective on what's happening, which is especially important since the people with whom a pastor chooses to share the most intimate details of his or her life must be limited. We must find ways to express feelings and release stress without alienating our loved ones—who, by the way, may be struggling with their own emotions over the situation. These dynamics will be examined more closely in the chapter "Home Is Where the Hurt Is." Just remember: when the garbage gets really deep, they'll be the ones most likely to grab a shovel. Blood is thicker than mud. Love covers a multitude of slime.

Maybe the hardest people to keep our cool with are those who exert a negative influence on our children's lives, such as an adult who should have known better than to say something harsh or hurtful or peers who support and even encourage our children's poor choices. They can be in or outside the church. Once during a Sunday evening service our middle son stood in response to a salvation message. It was a critical time when his own fragile identity was being weighed against his older brother's struggles. No sooner had he stood than a girl his age began whispering and harassing him, tugging on his arm until he sat down. Even knowing that if he was serious he should have had the courage to ignore her, I was furious.

But did I say anything? No, because we ministry models are not expected to express feelings the same way others do. Nor can we risk offending people and turning them away from the church. We're supposed to come up not only with just the right words but also with the divine response. In one of his humorous monologues, comedian Garrison Keillor laments the frustration of his fictional friar, Pastor Ingqvist, stating that, "when he bumps his knee on the corner of his desk, unlike others, the most satisfying words are just not available to him."

Yes, when things that we did not expect or invite come to invade our peaceful pastures, we set our sights for wolves. Simply put, we're looking for someone to shoot . . . or rather, blame. But we can't just blast away at every snapping twig and snipping remark. So with frayed nerves we sit on our stockpile of ammo. When the safety inevitably slips, there's only one safe direction for the exploding emotions to go: straight up.

One summer when our first two boys were very young, our family went to visit my parents in Wichita, Kansas. The first night a heavy rainstorm came through, thunder rolling like a bowling alley gone mad, fluorescent forks of lightning stabbing at the sky. Our older son, who was sleeping with us, had never in his three years seen or heard such a thing. Sitting straight up in bed, he cried, "Mommy, why is God doing this to us?" Even the next day he was hesitant to go outside in case he got "fundered" on.

Years later, when he no longer worried about the consequences of "funder" or anything else, I asked the same question: *God, why are You doing this to us?*

Even as ministers, we just can't help it. At some point, our hurting hearts turn heavenward, and we stand gazing up, desperate to see God looking back. By now we've asked Him a hundred times to intervene in our sad scenario, yet it seems He hasn't made a move. We're not, we remind Him, just any old body leaving a recorded message. We're the called, the committed, the clergy— the ones who have been faithful and made sacrifices. If anyone should have a heavenly hotline, it's us.

Oh, we know better than to blame God. We've read the Book of Job. But we've run out of places to direct the anger. Besides, we're more than a little hurt and confused. Is this the thanks we get for keeping the church up and running? Seems that since we were too busy to pay close attention to what was happening to our child, God should have. Or maybe He, too, looked away for just a moment and missed something.

Ever notice that the word "oops" is not in your Bible concordance? But you do find the names of a whole host of people whom God loved yet still charted their passage through some dire straits. Why? I see different reasons. Some, like Job, were good folks simply being tested. Others, like David, made mistakes and had to suffer the consequences of their own actions. And those poor prophets! God often seemed to use them just to make a point.

So what was that point? Whatever they were destined to endure, God had either a clear or clandestine plan or purpose. That's it. No other explanation. Sometimes they understood it; other times they didn't. God was challenging them to hang in there and trust Him. But note: they weren't just idly waiting for the outcome. God had purposed them as an active and integral part of it. And from those who persevered came the most practical, poignant, and poetic portions of Scripture. Their lives are a legacy of letters we devour now for insight and encouragement.

I wonder. Could someone be watching with interest for the next installment of our saga? One thing is clear: if God is to write a timeless epitaph on the pages of our lives, it's going to require that same sharp point.

Sharp point? Lord, we're being torn apart between You, our children, and the church. It's as if we're being crucified. Do You know what that's like?

Oh . . . yeah.

Maybe it's me. That's the thought that jump-starts the journey of a thousand regrets, a potentially long trek with incredibly heavy baggage, commonly known as a guilt trip. And it's no vacation. For months now we've been packing questions like *Where did we go wrong? Are we being punished? Why didn't we see this coming? How could we have been such horrible parents? Why didn't we make different decisions?*

Not far down the road we see the incriminating signs. Each, like the old Burma Shave ads (some of us are old enough to remember), leads to the next: "You tried to build fences" . . . "That your kid wouldn't vault" . . . "But he's over the edge now" . . . [big billboard] "SO IT MUST BE YOUR FAULT."

Screech. We've reached our destination.

Guilt, according to a description I received from a counselor friend, is anger turned inward. Still seeking guarantees? Here's one. Just look hard enough, long enough, and you'll find gallons to feel guilty about. There's a reason for that. You're human. No, worse: you're a human trying to be superhuman, also known as a minister.

Some of us don't even have to look that hard. One jangling wake-up call came for me during a recent discussion with my middle son. I had received an E-mail written by a family member we had loved but lost through divorce. It was filled with hurtful words expressing personal pain and anger. Most were general in nature or cited contributing circumstances. One ludicrous comment, however, was intentionally aimed in my direction. Reeling with shock, I said to my son, "Tell me honestly—did I do something to deserve this?"

"Mom"—was that a tinge of exasperation in his voice?—"it has nothing to do with you; but you'll find a way to take the blame somehow."

Blink.

Why would I do that? I don't want to be blamed or feel as if everything were my fault. Nor do I have a particularly poor self-image. I could only conclude that when there are no concrete answers, nothing specific we can put a finger on, it's just easier to take the blame, or blame others, than try to sort it all out.

But then, what if it *is* our fault and we just didn't see it coming?

Not long ago, after a quick trip to the shopping mall, I hopped in the car to leave. Backing out of the parking space, my eyes scanned for traffic in both directions. A vehicle had stopped on my right, waiting for me to pull out. At least I thought so. No sooner had I pressed my foot on the accelerator than I heard the staccato beeping of a horn, then a sickening thud. I had backed into the side of a midsize car stopped directly behind me.

Lower than the SUV I was driving—which, to make matters worse, belonged to my daughter-in-law—the small vehicle was out of my line of vision. I didn't want to file a claim with her insurance, so I apologetically exchanged information and agreed to reimburse the driver for repairs.

Afterward, of course, I kept replaying the scenario in my mind. How did this happen? It had not been intentional. How could it be my fault? But it was. I should have been paying closer attention and not been in such a hurry. Bottom line: I didn't see what was coming, but I'm paying dearly for it anyway.

I often feel that way about the situation with my children. If only I had been paying closer attention, things might have turned out differently. I wish I had known more, been less selfish, had a better perspective on life, seen the big picture. I wish, I wish, I wish.

In honest retrospect, we have a pretty good driving record as parents. Even our kids say so now. But we also made a few wrong turns, resulting in some obvious dings, dents, and damage. Welcome to the real world. So what do you do about it? There has to be a point on the condemnation compass where we stop blaming ourselves and begin trusting God to help us make the repairs, costly though they may be.

Listen pastoral partner: I can tell you from spending significant time there: Guilt Gulch is a dry and dusty place. So why are we tempted to revisit so often? Not only does every street take dangerous twists and turns—they're all dead ends. Hit the wall there, and you may never get out. Then it's only a stone's throw to Depression Desert.

Maybe you've heard this story. A man lying in bed says to his wife, "I'm not going to church today."

"Oh, yes, you are," she replies.

Pulling the covers over his head, he says, "I don't want to go, and you can't make me."

"Why don't you want to go?"

"The sermon is boring. And besides, I don't think those people like me very much."

The wife assumes a firm tone. "You have to go, and that's final."

Peeking out with one eye, he whines, "Give me one good reason why I should go."

"Because you're the pastor—that's why."

Humor is good medicine, according to Scripture. It can get us through some unbelievably tough times. Laughter relieves stress and helps us not to take ourselves or situations too seriously. However, should you wake up one morning truly unable to face the world, it's time to take inventory. Why? Depression is no laughing matter. And you're the pastor—that's why.

Many things contribute to depression. We're no longer in denial, which should be good news—unless we still struggle to accept what's happening and see little hope of immediate change. Our ongoing battle with anger has left us bone-weary, accomplishing nothing, and at times exacerbating the situation. We've also grown tired of blaming others. Besides, assigning fault hasn't fixed anything. We try to trust that God is in control, all the while wondering how long our prayers will hover in that heavenly holding pattern. So many hopes for our child are dashed, and our family is fractured. Our personal guilt trip has taken us farther than we wanted to go. Now we feel guilty about being depressed, prompting yet another gallop around the gulch.

Whoa, Nelly!

Everyone has occasional bouts of depression, especially when going through life-altering circumstances. To say that ministers should never get depressed is to say that doctors should never get sick. Still, folks frown on either bringing it to the office with them. It could be contagious.

Truth is, ministers are rather good at hiding the symptoms and managing life around these bouts. After all, we have to keep the parish plates spinning, whether or not we feel like it. In one way that's not a bad thing. It keeps us in contact with people and involved in daily life, so we don't dwell on our problems or withdraw, a symptom often typical of depression.

But busyness can also become an escape. Faster and faster we run, hoping to stay ahead or avoid the problem, all the while postponing, or worse, exacerbating the situation. Our overt involvement may simply reinforce the common complaint of prodigals that ministry takes precedence over family. It may also leave the other spouse to carry a larger part of the burden, which creates resentment and adds to the stress at home. No matter how clever your cover at church, depression can be lurking in the dark corners just outside the sanctuary doors, waiting to hitch a ride home.

No wonder we end up feeling as if we're living a double life, even worrying that our situation may constitute a double standard. Then, fearing accusations of duplicity, spiritual weakness, or lack of faith, we may do the very worst thing: minimize our feelings or suppress them entirely. The results can be disastrous: a full-blown depression that's defeating and debilitating, maybe even affecting our health.

James Margolis, a psychiatrist with Sutter Health, a local agency, says, "We feel our emotions through our physical being. When someone has a major loss and talks about his or her heart being broken, the person can actually feel it in his or her chest."

"That can't happen," you say. "Not to us theological tough guys."

As I was writing this chapter, a headline in our local newspaper caught my attention: "Grief's Emotions Can Also Have Physical Effect." The article was, in part, about well-known San Francisco Giants baseball player Barry Bonds. Here's what it said:

Even tough guys get the blues.

Last week, grief over his father's death decked Barry Bonds, one of the best baseball players of all time and a man known for his nerves of steel and his emotional stoicism. Bonds, his breathing labored and his heart racing at a dangerous clip, left the field and ended up in the hospital. Doctors said stress over the death of his dad, Bobby, likely caused the symptoms.

Although the San Francisco Giants superstar's reaction was more dramatic than most, it offers powerful proof of the connection between the mind and physical health, experts said.

"A guy like Barry Bonds might feel the need to get back out there, to be tough, to help his team get ready for the playoffs," said Kathy Marty, a licensed clinical social worker. . . . "That might be fine, but it might also add to the pressure and help contribute to physical symptoms. It doesn't mean he's a weak man. Even though he's a strong, professional athlete, he's entitled to his grief."[1]

Could it be that we strong, spiritual professionals are also entitled to our grief, especially if God happens to be using the dearest thing to us—our children—to teach us some valuable life lessons?

To grieve, to acknowledge emotions, is not to be weak. Nor, in the case of ministers, is it unspiritual. A normal range of emotion is part of the natural process in coming to grips with any difficult circumstance. As a pastor's wife, I learned early the necessity of allowing myself to grieve when transition required me to leave a beloved home and congregation. Otherwise I could never have fully embraced the next. But emotions out of control can render us ineffective, even be counterproductive to God's work in our lives and those of our children. So how do we continue to function without being overwhelmed, embittered, or paralyzed by them?

Any student of Scripture knows—it's all in the translation.

Recently I decided to read again through the New Testament using Eugene Peterson's brilliant Bible translation, *The Message*. In his introduction chapter, Peterson talks about how the books of the New Testament came to be written and arranged. They were written in the street language of the day—informal Greek—which comes as a surprise, he says, to some who think "holy things should be elevated—stately and ceremonial." I love the way he describes it instead as "a rough and earthy language that reveals

God's presence and action where we least expect it." Then he speaks of his own goal to translate it not into a "word-for-word conversion of Greek to English" but rather "into the way we actually think and speak."

Now read his final paragraph, one that speaks to the heart of every minister.

In the midst of doing this work, I realized that this is exactly what I have been doing all my vocational life. For thirty-five years as a pastor I stood at the border between two languages, biblical Greek and everyday English, acting as a translator, providing the right phrases, getting the right words so that the men and women to whom I was pastor could find their way around and get along in the world where God has spoken so decisively and clearly in Jesus. I did it from the pulpit and in the kitchen, in hospitals and restaurants, on parking lots and at picnics, always looking for an English way to make the biblical text relevant to the conditions of the people.

What about we who are standing on the border between the church and our much-loved children, children who have made poor choices that affect all of us? Like it or not, this is where we're living. Can we find a way to translate spiritually what's happening on the most personal and poignant level of our lives to our congregation and others? If so, I believe it will speak more personally to people than anything we say in a Sunday School class or behind a pulpit. God is giving us a chance not just to teach people but also to reach people, while redeeming our own families in the process.

"But," you say, "I'm having a hard time translating this for myself. Not every ministry family goes through this struggle with their children. Is it because they did something right and we did something wrong? We must've already blown it, or we wouldn't be going through this now."

How do you know that?

Donnie Moore is a dynamic youth evangelist who has been a great friend to our family. Many years ago he said something in a sermon that I jotted down in the front of my Bible and quote often. He said, "Circumstances don't reveal who we will become as much as they reveal who we already are." Maybe you don't like the person who has been revealed through your particular set of circumstances. On the other hand, you could be surprised at how well you've weathered the storm. Either way, we surely learn a lot about ourselves in the process, don't we? And we learn even more about how God sees us. After all these years of believing Him, it's both amazing and humbling to realize that He also believes in us.

Having written that, I can't resist throwing in one more well-known quote attributed to the late Mother Teresa: "I know God will never place anything on me that I can't bear. I just wish He didn't trust me so much." Amen, Sister.

So does this mean we'll never again struggle with a mixed myriad of emotions? No, we will. Some days will still be harder than others, and we'll react humanly. But hopefully as our outlook changes, our responses will, too. In the meantime, remember: it's never too late for attitude adjustments and apologies.

From His own word, we know it's not God's desire that any, including our precious prodigals, should perish. He never stops seeking, so we must never stop praying and believing for their safe return. We come to see it not as celestial crisis but divine design. Look closely, and you might even find the label: "Custom made in heaven for [fill in your name]."

Heaven knows what has happened in our children's lives. But rest assured: God is not just present—He's active in all our lives. More is happening in the heavenly realm than we can possibly know.

This means coming to see our situation not as punishment but as a journey God will make with us. That requires us, then, to make a choice as to whether we'll allow our emotions to overwhelm us, making us bitter and disillusioned, or filter them through prayer and the Word.

By doing the latter, we free ourselves to move ahead, committed not just to fulfilling our duty to ministry—this is way bigger than that—but also to our devotion to living out God's heavenly purpose on earth. And like any good father, He promises a gift to keep us going. His peace passes earthly understanding.

Only then will our question no longer be "What in heaven's name has happened?" but "How will God use us for heaven's sake?"

Lord, we're trying hard to trust Your greater purpose. In the process we've run the gamut of emotion. We're none too proud of some of them, either. Help us in this dash of destiny not to be over-

whelmed or undermined. We know that feelings have nothing to do with faith. But it still seems easier to believe on some days than on others. Help us to remember that You're with us on both days. Touch us, Lord, in heart, mind, and emotion. Help us see through Your eyes so You may shine through ours. In Your name we pray. Amen.

It would be so much easier—wouldn't it—if we could pinpoint what caused our children to walk out the sanctuary doors with no intention of returning. *If we can just figure it out,* we reason, *perhaps we can fix it.* But as already discussed, it's much more complicated than that.

There's no denying it: ministers' kids sometimes get caught in the crossfire of church problems and hurtful circumstances. It can't always be avoided. And while getting a handle on our own emotions goes a long way toward helping them not to return fire, a lot still depends on the child. Some are much more easily disillusioned and susceptible to negative influence. And don't think for a minute that the devil doesn't know that. Without doubt, this treacherous traitor aims his arrows where they'll do the most damage.

Before relating any more of our own personal prodigal story, I feel it's important that we take a chapter to reestablish who our real enemy is. Not that I have any desire to give Satan credit. Rather, my hope is to discredit his diabolical deeds in order to help us focus our emotional energy where it will do the most good.

When those fiery darts start flying, exposing the source may help us position our shields of faith and keep collateral damage to a minimum.

3

Collateral Damage

Guard the good deposit that was entrusted to you;
guard it with the help of the Holy Spirit who lives in us.
—2 Tim. 1:4

It is August 1992. The late morning fog is just beginning to lift in a small North Bay town near San Francisco. As Pastor Dan Elledge sits alone in his third-floor church office studying for the evening Bible class, a tap sounds on the door . . . one that will soon echo in eternity.

"Come on in," Dan calls. He expects it to be the music minister, who is already late for their midmorning meeting. Instead, a stranger enters. In broken English he asks if he might have a drink of water.

Must be a worker who's wandered in from outside, Dan assumes. "Sure, wait right here." He walks down the hall to the kitchen.

Reentering his office with the water, he finds the man holding a handgun. The intention is obvious: robbery. Reacting instinctively, Dan tries to overpower him, at which point a second accomplice rushes in. Deadly danger registers and the young pastor attempts to flee. Both men fire, then rush to finish what they came for.

Minutes later an eyewitness sees the two men leaving the scene carrying church equipment. Suspicious, he calls police on his car phone. A chase ensues and they are arrested a few blocks away. The goods are recovered, but something of much greater value has been taken. The police, along with the late-arriving music minister, find Dan Elledge crumpled on the landing of an outside staircase, dead from his wounds.

That afternoon his wife, Gail, struggling to contain her own grief and disbelief, has to tell their 7-year-old son, Andrew, that Daddy is in heaven. The thieves who took Dan Elledge's life left his wife and young, impressionable son to suffer the collateral damage.

"Collateral damage" is a military term. The combined words are commonly used to describe people or structures affected or destroyed as the result of something else that was targeted, usually by a bomb or some other weapon. Between current world conflicts and escalating terrorism, it is a term we have become chillingly familiar with. "Collateral damage" is what Timothy McVeigh called the children who died when he bombed the federal building in Oklahoma City. Though convicted and executed as the diabolical detonator of that horrible explosion, we know McVeigh was only an accomplice.

The real perpetrator has slithered his way from Eden through the ages. Peter warned the first-century church "Be self-controlled and alert. Your enemy the devil prowls around like a roaring lion looking for someone to devour" (1 Pet. 5:8). In the 15th century, Martin Luther penned this phrase in his classic hymn, "A Mighty Fortress Is Our God": "for still our ancient foe, doth seek to work us woe." All are words now echoing into the 21st-century Church as we stand on the front lines of spiritual battle alerting people to his schemes and tactics. There is no doubt that we, too, will be targets of his attacks. The question is, how can we keep our families from becoming collateral damage?

Thank God, not every prodigal parable carries the spiraling repercussions of a pastor being shot in his own church. Yet we all know of those who have suffered unexpected, unexplainable trauma. In a more symbolic sense, however, many a pastor's reputation is assassinated daily by those seeking to find fault and rob him of integrity. Our spiritual life is often on the line, and sometimes our children get caught in the crossfire. Any impressionable child will struggle to understand God allowing his or her parent to be so wounded.

Pastors themselves struggle in coming to terms with personal traumas, attacks, and disappointments. It's when their guard is down that a number succumb to unfortunate temptations and indiscretions. Sad to say, we hear of moral failures in ministry more frequently than ever before. More often, however, the confusion and bitterness surface through some internal conflict, the most common being with staff, board, or congregational members. Latent insecurities and personal unhappiness manifest themselves in many ways. The result is that some walk away from ministry under a dark cloud of disgrace, doubt, and disillusionment. Sadly, their children are soured or scarred by the parent's own shortcomings.

Whatever form these attacks of the enemy take, the results seem to vary widely depending on how we choose to return fire. In some cases we can disarm him if we will only take time to consider our reactions prayerfully and carefully. Other situations, however, are unavoidable. Sometimes we don't even find out until after the damage is done. Then we must ask God for divine words and wisdom to interpret the harsh realities of life.

There are, however, some preventive measures we can take to protect our children from words and actions that are potentially hurtful.

Let's admit it. Even we exegetical experts tussle at times with the sacred trust. Ever have one—or a hundred—of those days when you wonder why you ever chose to enter ministry in the first place? We all have. Oh, maybe not ministry in its entirety. Just some small, irritating aspect of it. Like one honest pastor who said, "Ministry is great! It's the people I can't stand." We know from experience that these chafing chapters come, scripturally speaking, to pass. But our children don't have that kind of overview. Until they do pass, here's a word of caution. Those are probably not the best times to express or explain anything about ministry to them. Some days the best wisdom is to keep a tight lip and go hit a few golf balls. Or take up kick boxing.

Even on the good days we know it's prudent to be careful how much of the ministry business we bring home. We *know.* But we still do it. After all, home is where we lose the liturgy and cast off the clerical collar. It's a natural place to verbally process the stress. We've all been guilty of revealing too much information about certain situations or people over the dinner table, only to have it come back and bite us. As one pastor lamented, "I should have spent as much time relating the positive events as I did the problems with people." If we want our children to reflect a healthy attitude toward ministry, it pays to handpick the words we feed them.

Then sometimes kids just hear things incorrectly. One day when our boys were still small a neighbor came to my door, laughing her head off. "I just overheard a conversation between our kids," she gasped between giggles. "What your son said was priceless."

Uh-oh, I thought. *Now what?*

It seems the kids were discussing religion and one little girl had just announced she was Catholic. Then, turning to my son, she asked, "What are you?"

"I dunno," he said, "but I think we're prostitutes."

Careful as we might be to guard our conversation, kids—even the youngest ones—are more perceptive than we think. But good perception doesn't guarantee correct processing.

Unfortunately we cannot always predict how our children will process or react to negative situations. It seems that most adverse reactions involving ministry result not from just one incident but many combined over a period of time. And, yes, these often seem to include some conscious or unconscious action on our part. Sad to say, by the time we figure it out, our children may have already walked out and slammed the gate.

Friends, there's no getting around it. Satan is out to destroy God's people, particularly those in leadership. Though many stories I received from past prodigals indicate that the first seeds of rebellion sprouted because they felt their feelings and opinions were ignored or minimized, or that their pastor-parents cared more about the church than them, it soon becomes obvious there was a distinct point and time when any number of Satan-inspired circumstances and outside influences also came into play. Then it's as if they crossed some imaginary line and there was no turning back.

There is one interesting thing to note. Though the reasons children from ministry families rebel are many and varied, in most cases when prodigals "come to their senses," few end up blaming their parent for the poor decisions they made. In fact most indicate that it was the parent's unconditional love and support during those difficult years that drew them back.

Frankly, some kids are so impressionable that nothing we do can prevent them from a rebellious reaction. But it may help to remember this: rebellion can be just an angry attempt to get questions answered honestly. It doesn't mean they are lost forever. In his book *Good News About Prodigals,*[1] Tom Bisset suggests that faith rejection is more about searching for truth than it is about rejecting truth. At that point it has become the child's own spiritual battle.

Remember Paul, the son of our missionary friends, from the last chapter? I believe the rest of his story serves as a good illustration.

Following that troubling transmission to his parents in Africa, it took several years of "doing his own thing" before Paul finally acknowledged he was in trouble. His grades suffered to the point of academic probation, then dismissal; he became physically involved in several romantic relationships, and he started using alcohol as an escape from spiritual conviction.

"I set off to find myself and got lost along the way," Paul says now. "Yet I have no doubt that my soul was subconsciously crying out to God."

No doubt indeed. Because halfway around the world Paul's parents, concerned for his immediate safety and eternal welfare, prayed urgently. It's easy to see that they recognized the real enemy by the weapon they chose to battle him. And it worked. The more they prayed the more things intensified in Paul's life.

"God placed many people in my life during that time who made a huge difference," Paul recalls. This included an old friend named Todd, someone who knew the pre-prodigal Paul. One late October night they went for a drive and ended up talking for hours about life and God. And so it was, as they sat in the cab of Todd's truck, that a simple prayer along with a lot of tears brought Paul back into the fold of grace.

Now he's making up for lost time. Working hard to advance his education, he plans to eventually teach in a Bible college or seminary.

Undoubtedly someone is reading this and thinking, *That's wonderful. But you don't understand the damage in my child's life. It's too late to change what has happened, and the outcome at this point seems questionable at best.*

True, for many of us it's too late for prevention. But it's never too late for redemption. Though the devil may seem to have won a skirmish or two, the battle is still the Lord's.

And you are not alone. Many of us are still fighting and binding up the wounds. Once again Peter's words echo from the walls of that first-century Church to encourage us: "Resist him [the devil], standing firm in the faith, because you know that your brothers throughout the world are undergoing the same kind of sufferings" (1 Pet. 5:9).

And what about Andrew, the boy who was 7 years old when his father was shot and killed? Due to the devastating events, his mother, Gail, wisely sought immediate professional counseling for him. Her main concern: "He didn't cry for a long time." She eventually remarried a wonderful man who is also a minister. Someone committed to understanding the long-term effects on such a young, impressionable child. Their ministry eventually took them far from the San Francisco Bay area—but for Andrew, not far enough from the memories. You see, he had been with his dad for a while on that fateful morning but accepted an invitation to go play at a friend's house just before the attack took place. It has been difficult for him to surrender his 7-year-old conviction that if he'd stayed he might have somehow saved his dad.

Now 18 and in his last year of high school, Andrew's mom believes he is close to finally sorting out the pieces of his past. Her continuing prayer is that it will positively shape his future and his faith.

What better place to be reminded of the culmination of Joseph's story recorded in Gen. 50:20? "You intended to harm me," Joseph says to his brothers. "But God intended it for good to accomplish what is now being done, the saving of many lives." And it's still true today. What the enemy means for evil, God can still ultimately use for good.

Lord, we pray right now for every pastor's child adversely affected by some negative experience or circumstance of ministry. We bind the power of the enemy that seeks to destroy. You know the confusion and the pain, the anger and hurt. Minister to them. Bring someone alongside who will understand and encourage. Whisper help into those empty spaces in their hearts. Administer healing to their open wounds. Cover their scars with Your own nail-scarred hand. In Your name we pray. Amen.

We are so prone to wanting every story to have a happy ending. But if you notice, stories with happy endings nearly always involve some conflict, which only makes us cheer louder when the good guys win. The important thing is not to lose hope or perspective in the process.

Fact is, some of us are still living in the middle of the book. If today you're pondering circumstances that seem to be out of control, let me encourage you once again. God is on our side, and more is happening in the heavenly realm than we can see.

In the meantime, the last thing we should do is just sit on our earthly inertia. Not when His Word provides a detailed diagram to prepare us for battle.

4

Battle Plan

*The weapons we fight with are not the weapons
of the world. On the contrary, they have
divine power to demolish strongholds.*
—2 Cor. 10:4

No matter how the war against rebellion rages, we don't have to sit helplessly by waiting to see what the outcome will be. We're in this battle together. Let's determine to focus our energy on the real enemy, arming ourselves daily with the weapons divinely designed for his defeat. For that purpose, let's review a familiar battle plan laid out in Eph. 6:12-18.

"For our struggle," Paul writes, "is not against flesh and blood, but against the rulers, against the authorities, against the powers of this dark world and against the spiritual forces of evil in the heavenly realms" (v. 12).

Somehow this reminds me of a bumper sticker I once saw: *Just because we're paranoid, it doesn't mean they're not out to get us.* Yes, Scripture makes it clear: we have a very real enemy who is out to get us. But rather than being paranoid, let's be prepared. I believe Paul begins with this statement because to battle effectively there must be no confusion about who the real enemy is. Especially in the heat of battle, it's a crucial point. Our child is not our enemy, or our church, or even those who hurt us, whether it's deliberate or not. Our enemy is Satan, who wants to discourage and defeat us from pursuing God and accomplishing His will. He'll find ways to come against us physically, mentally, and emotionally. At those times we must find a way to protect ourselves spiritually. Not only the lives of our family members depend on it, but also the lives of those we influence through ministry depend on it.

"Therefore put on the full armor of God," Paul says, "so that when the day of evil comes, you may be able to stand your ground, and after you have done everything, to stand" (v. 13).

Notice He says "when" the day of evil comes, not "if." In every life there will be days that seem incredibly diabolic, when we've done everything we know to do. Never mind standing our ground —we're blessed to be standing at all. So how do we stay on our feet? By doing what our mothers always taught us. Before you ever go out the door in the morning, be sure you're dressed right.

"Stand firm then, with the belt of truth buckled around your waist, with the breastplate of righteousness in place" (v. 14).

Can you even imagine being able to sit in armor? Still there's a distinct difference between standing weak-kneed and wobbly and standing firm. This scripture seems to indicate that the key may be in tightening up that truth belt a notch or two.

Someone once said that truth is always its own best defense. In other words, if we're on the side of right, we don't have to worry about what anyone lobs at us. However, in the confusion of battle it's sometimes possible for the lines to get a little blurry. No proper pastor would deliberately do anything dishonest; but we will all be tempted at some point to compromise for the sake of peace. We have to know how far we can bend without breaking God's law if we're to be able to communicate it clearly to our children. Buckle up. Know God's Word, and wrap it snugly around you. Literally speaking, the belt of truth keeps our spiritual pants up. Then we're not so apt to stumble on the path of righteousness.

And how do we keep that breastplate of righteousness in place? By checking daily to ensure our relationship with the Lord hasn't shifted. Should we discover a ding, it's critical to make immediate repairs. Why? It's the one piece of armor that guards our heart.

Now that we're standing firm, Paul draws attention to our feet: "and with your feet fitted with the readiness that comes from the gospel of peace" (v. 15).

A couple of years ago I was asked to speak for Mother's Day services at a large local church. Using Prov. 22:6 as my text, I talked about what I call the "time-released principle" of Christian training, how the "seeds" we plant in our children, like physical seeds, don't always bloom in the time or way we expect. As an illustration, I made a brief but emotional reference to my own children.

After the service a lady approached me. "I just wanted to tell you," she said with a shy smile, "that you have beautiful feet."

I looked down, assuming she was complimenting my shoes. Then she continued. "You know the scripture that says 'How beautiful are the feet of those who bring good news!' I really needed some good news today. You gave me hope." Then she said it again: "You have beautiful feet."

It was the best compliment I've ever received, one I'll never forget.

No matter what your circumstances, always be ready to carry the gospel of peace to others. From the depth of our own "sole" struggles come the very words that may encourage someone else, even on the days when you must keep reminding yourself to put one beautiful foot in front of the other.

"In addition to all this, take up the shield of faith, with which you can extinguish all the flaming arrows of the evil one" (v. 16).

Ching. Whizzz. Cha-ching. Some days those fiery darts fly fast and furious. Approaching burnout, a thought sears our spirits: *I'm not sure I have enough faith for this.* Now I ask you, is there a way to measure faith? And if we could, would it still be faith? Elton Trueblood said, "Faith is not belief without proof, but trust without reservation." I don't know Mr. Trueblood, but that's an insightful definition. My husband, who I do know, observes that most people start asking for more faith before they've begun to use what they already have. Or if you want my take, even a mustard seed won't grow until you stick it into the dirt.

Shields up, shepherds!

"Take the helmet of salvation and the sword of the Spirit, which is the word of God" (v. 17).

If the devil can get us to doubt who we are in Christ, then defeat is imminent. Can that happen to those who minister to others? Perhaps, if we entertain thoughts like these long enough: *Do you see what your kid is doing? Who did he learn that from? You really blew it this time. How can you call yourself a Christian, much less a minister?* To plant that kind of doubt, the enemy has to get inside our heads. See something symbolic here?

Knowing that one of the enemy's greatest battlefields is on the fertile soil of our minds, the apostle Paul suggests in his second letter to the Corinthians that we take a few prisoners of war. "We demolish arguments and every pretension that sets itself up against the knowledge of God," he instructs, "and we take captive every thought to make it obedient to Christ" (2 Cor. 10:5). We know to whom we belong. Let's chase down those demons of doubt and make 'em POWs.

Should we ever be in danger of losing our heavenly head-gear—or our heads, for that matter—all we have to do is pull out the Sword. God's Word applied in the Spirit's strength will defeat every devilish maneuver. It worked for Jesus, friend. And it will work for us.

"And pray in the Spirit on all occasions with all kinds of prayers and requests. With this in mind, be alert and always keep on pray-ing for all the saints" (v. 18).

Prayer is the weapon we can use any time, any place. Why is it sometimes the last one we draw? Maybe we just don't know what to say. Or we find ourselves repeating the same pathetic plea. Or maybe someone with a hissing lisp has convinced us that it isn't working.

Snap out of it!

Absorb Paul's pep talk to the Ephesians. You're not praying alone. You're praying in Dolby stereo. Imagine your prayers, in-spired and directed by the Holy Spirit, bouncing and echoing around the walls of heaven. Paul seems to be telling us not to wait for a special occasion to pray. Pray at all times in all ways. Say whatever comes to mind. Then be alert, not just for the enemy's rustle but even the faintest whisper from heaven.

And while you're at it, remember to pray for others.

Lord, Your Word says that the battle belongs to You. We claim that promise right now. We come against the enemy of our souls by arming ourselves with the knowledge of Your Word. We don't want to duel through another day without Your protective armor. Whatever the enemy launches our way, help us defend our ground. We've read the last chapter, and we know who wins. Help us fight like conquerors and claim victory in the name of the King! In Your name we pray. Amen.

Now we've pegged the enemy and polished the armor. I feel better—don't you? Perhaps, with this perspective, it won't be as difficult to peruse a few more personally painful pages.

5

Raw Pain

*I pour out my complaint before him; before him
I tell my trouble; When my spirit grows faint within me,
it is you who know my way.*
—Ps. 142:2-3

*Dear Mom and Dad, I am realizing day by day that there's
something really wrong with me. The unknown anger and frustration seem to rule me. I don't understand it. It's starting to ruin this family. Though I'm scared to admit it, I really think I should see a psychiatrist or someone who can help me, because I'm growing scared of myself. I can't control anything happening to me. It's tearing me up, and that comes out on you. I know I've caused a lot of problems and turmoil in this family. I never meant to hurt either of you, yet it seems I have a great ability for causing pain.*

Pain—such a small word to describe something so all-consuming! A friend with her own prodigal son once described it as "carrying a rock in your heart." I want to tell you that after we received this note from our son, we got him the help he needed, and the pain went away.

I want to. But I can't.

As I look back, the thing that still amazes me is how swiftly and violently things fell apart. For three years his performance in school deteriorated steadily, grade-wise and every other-wise. Skipping school and getting into fights became his regular routine. By this time he had attended three different public high schools, done a short stint in a Christian school, and tried a couple of alternative learning centers. In the first semester of his junior year he gave up and dropped out altogether.

After that he picked up a few short-lived jobs, mostly for spending money. One, which he secured through the employment agency I worked for at the time, was with a well-known department store. The day my boss called me in to tell me my son had been detained on suspicion of robbing the register, I felt like the one caught with my hand in the till. Would we ever be able to stop answering for this kid's bad decisions?

Around this same time his personality began to change drastically. He became more verbally abusive and physically aggressive. Our attempts to keep him at home resulted not just in arguments but in actual battles. How can I ever forget the night Jim tried to physically restrain him and the scuffle that ensued? By the time he left, walls shuddering as the door banged behind him, his brothers had retreated to their rooms, I sat on the floor sobbing, and Jim stood holding on to a chair, trying to regain his composure.

Sometimes he would pretend to comply with our wishes, then wait until we were asleep and leave. It wasn't unusual for him to disappear for two or three days at a time without making contact. In all honesty, our home atmosphere was so tense when he was around that it was a reprieve when he was gone. Except that we worried, not knowing where he was, whether he would make it home or in what condition. More and more, home was becoming a place he came to shower, get clean clothes, and crash. As his behavior grew more irrational, we had little doubt that he had begun taking drugs. Time proved us right.

The drugs combined with his anger and confusion to produce a completely self-absorbed stranger. *This is what I want,* his actions screamed, *and if you don't give it to me, I'll take it anyway.* Problem was, he didn't know what he wanted. We knew his erratic behavior was an outward symbol of terrible inward turmoil, that somewhere under the pain still lived the son we loved and who loved us back. Though everything spoke to the contrary, there was no doubt he hated himself for hurting us. Another note he wrote during this time expresses it clearly.

Mom and Dad, I can't give explanations for my actions. I'm sorry that I lose control. I hate it when I lose my mind. Thank you for trying and for your love. I don't know where I would be right now if it weren't for your effort. I hope I can make up for the pain I cause you guys at times. I love you, and I'm trying.

I believe he did try at times. But he was relying on his own strength. Somehow he just couldn't let go of the lifestyle and give the controls back to God. And every time he failed and slipped back, we watched his self-confidence erode a bit more. As a result, he was a seething bundle of contradictions, trapping us all on a roller coaster ride of angry outbursts, tearful tirades, apathetic apologies, and broken promises.

I never did like roller coasters.

His poor choices made it almost impossible for us to agree or find compromises. We could not give his lifestyle approval nor would he allow us to serve any longer as his conscience. In his determination to run his own life, he was backing himself into a corner. It was apparent we were headed for an inevitable parting of the ways. The only question was "When?" Hard as circumstances were, we tried to postpone it. We knew that once he left home we would lose what little influence and control we still had. Besides, he was not quite 17, and we were still legally responsible.

Then two substantial straws settled on the sagging camel's back.

I received a phone call informing me that my mother, who was battling Parkinson's disease back in the Midwest, had been hospitalized and could be released only to a nursing home. On top of that, my dad, exhausted from caring for her, had developed pneumonia. We knew the time had come to bring my parents to California so we could assist in their care. Within three weeks, we had Mom settled into a care facility near our house, and Dad was sharing a room with our youngest son. How could things possibly get anymore complicated? We soon found out.

It seems our oldest son had now gravitated toward a new group of playmates, a gang called skinheads. These were people— some were his age but a number were older—who provided a violent venue for his all-consuming anger under the guise of their own misguided cause. He had finally found an identity—one that couldn't have been farther removed from ours. Helpless, we watched him drift into a haze of hate with a sickening certainty that we couldn't build a bridge fast enough to span the ever-widening chasm.

The picture we had taken for the church directory that year captured the contrast clearly. Jim is wearing the pastor's standard-issue suit and tie; I'm a well-coiffured-and-coordinated fashion plate; our youngest son portrays the typical gap-toothed ten-year-old; our middle son has hair down to his shoulders; and our oldest son has no hair at all. Sadly, it would be the last, least-memorable picture taken of our original five-piece family.

That directory symbolizes another interesting irony. Thin as we were being stretched at home, the church was thriving. Somehow, with God's help, we managed to apportion our energies and compartmentalize our ministry. Our congregation had more than doubled in size, giving us much-needed affirmation that someone was embracing our teaching, even if it wasn't our own children. There's no doubt that our congregation's great love and personal ministry got us through those trying years. Like the directory, it kept us connected.

Only because of our church family are there a number of warm, fuzzy photos intermingled in my book of memories from that time. These include Christmas open houses and special events, the last few family gatherings with my parents still in the picture, and a couple of memorable trips the church funded so Jim and I could temporarily escape the stress.

Then there are the torn pages, faded fragments of the devastating direction our son's life was taking. There was nothing to do but hold on and pray. And pray we did.

It would take a separate book to record all the ensuing incidents. Many we never knew in detail; nor would I want to. But I could almost tell you when they happened, judging by the number of times I was awakened in the middle of the night with an urgency to fall on my knees. I know God intervened in ways we'll never realize this side of heaven. And our son knew it, too. "You had to be praying, Mom," he's confirmed more than once. "Otherwise I wouldn't be here now."

Take for instance the night we received the frantic phone call asking his dad to come pick him up.

"Where are you?" Jim asked.

"I'm not sure . . . just a minute." Mumbled voices in the background, then sketchy directions. When Jim finally located the place, he got the whole story from our obviously shaken son. It seems he was leaving a party and had been jumped by an opposing gang of skinheads. He managed to escape and run for his life, ending up a few blocks away at the house of a guy Jim later described as looking like a Hell's Angels member. Why that fellow let our son in and took the risk of getting involved, I don't know. We can only believe God temporarily turned a Hell's Angels member into a guardian angel that night—further proving my theory that God works in "mischievous" ways His wonders to perform.

I wonder—how many times, in the distress of just wanting the pain to end, did we neglect to be thankful? There were so many times I know our worst-case scenarios provided a proving ground for God's faithfulness. And we didn't even take the time to acknowledge it.

Lord, we are truly grateful.

One of the things I'm most thankful for is that somehow during those years our youngest son managed to stay above the fray. Too young to be interested in the same friends and activities as his brothers, he was pretty much into doing his own thing. Strange as it may seem, he enjoyed having my dad as a roommate. Being together in that situation, they developed a much closer relationship than he and the other two boys did. Truth is, our youngest son reminds me a lot of my dad. Even today, when he walks into a room with his baseball hat turned slightly sideways or speaks in a certain tone of voice, I feel a nostalgic tug.

That doesn't mean he didn't see and hear what was going on around him. It just didn't negatively affect his behavior at the time. Though he went through his own short form of rebellion later on, I believe seeing so many of the negative consequences from that distance positively shaped many of his future opinions and choices—resulting in his ultimate decision to serve God.

Our middle son, however, was particularly close to his older brother. Only two years apart in age, neither could remember a time when the other wasn't there. It was natural for them to want to do things together, and they shared many of the same friends and activities. To their credit, there were times they kept each other out of trouble. But there were also times they waded knee-deep into it together. It was only as our oldest son began to embrace the skinhead scene that our middle son decided he might be getting in over his head. But instead of getting out of the current, he let it take him in a different direction.

The night my dad got up to use the bathroom and found him passed out drunk, curled around the toilet, was when we realized we were dealing with not just one set of problems but two. It would only be a few months later that he and his girlfriend sat together in our living room informing us she was pregnant. They were both 16. My husband sat stunned, but he assured them of our support. All I could do was cry. He told us later that she had miscarried, but we were never sure if that was the truth. To our discredit, we never bothered to find out. At that point we simply had more than we could handle.

Close as they were, I always found it interesting that our middle son resented having his bad behavior blamed on his older brother's example. I guess, being the middle child, he wanted to establish that his problems were unique, not just a copy of someone else's. A point he managed to prove well for a number of years.

Lord, what did we do to deserve such pain? It's a question we've all cried out to God. I can only conclude that, like God, we chose to have children—children with free will and full reign to make their own choices, children who never meant to hurt us but became so caught up and confused by their own personal conflict that they stopped caring about the effects their behavior had on others.

Enter then the enemy.

He always comes with some variation of the same lisping lie used to snare Eden's pair. *Boundaries are bad. They only want to keep you from knowing, being, doing. Break the rules, and you'll be free.* Too late they discover that's when the real bondage begins, and with it the pain of personal loss and failure for all involved.

Two lines from a poem our oldest son wrote at some point in the pain says it all. It's entitled "Paying the Piper":

Be careful what you wish for—you might just get it.

Be careful what you wish for—you might just regret it.

Why is it that children allow themselves to be so influenced by those who obviously care little about their well-being rather than listening to the counsel of those who love them so much? We can't help but take it personally. It's the worst form of betrayal. No wonder the pain can be incapacitating.

Perhaps it's even more so for those who don't see it coming.

Music ministry was Nancy Decker's calling at the church in Colorado where she and her husband, Ed, attended. Their daughter played flute in the orchestra and had been a model child. Jamie came home when she was told or called if she was going to be late. Actively involved in church, she had many achievements to her credit and seemed to enjoy life. After high school graduation, she found a well-paying job with a national restaurant chain. When she decided to get an apartment with a girlfriend, her parents gave their blessing, having no reason to believe that she wouldn't be fine. Soon, however, they began to notice some troubling changes.

She didn't come to church as often, was growing more distant, and had begun dating a boy from work. They were crushed to learn that she had started smoking. It was when Jamie discovered that her boyfriend and her own roommate had become sexually involved that things took a serious turn. Within months she informed her parents that she was taking her grandmother's inheritance of $16,000 and moving to San Francisco—with a boy she had known for one month.

"I cried, prayed, and tried to talk her out of it," Nancy says. "I tried to explain why this was wrong according to Scripture." But to no avail.

The truck with 170,000 miles on it that Jamie bought to make the trip got them to Los Angeles before breaking down. Within three months the young fugitives had spent all of her inheritance (sound like a familiar story from the Bible?) and were living at Venice Beach in the back of the truck. Her boyfriend couldn't keep a job, so Jamie went back to work for her old restaurant chain, a two-hour bus commute each way.

For a year, her parents' only contact with their daughter was by phone. Following one call in which Jamie sounded extremely depressed and desperate, her dad decided to try to find her. It was literally a miracle when he spotted her and the boyfriend walking down the street. For a week her father tried to convince her. Then came the predictable prodigal pronouncement: "I got myself into this mess, and I'll get myself out."

At home her mother interceded in prayer, crying out in pain to the Lord. When her husband called to say Jamie wasn't coming, she couldn't believe it. "I can't describe the feelings," she says. "Rejection, hurt, anger—all the negative emotions one can feel. I didn't understand why God would let me down. I had served Him, worked for Him, praised and worshiped Him. I couldn't help feeling totally rejected by God." She would have resigned her music ministry then, but her wise pastor's wife wouldn't let her.

"Week after week I walked out onto the platform only to see the orchestra chair where Jamie should have been sitting," she recalls. "All I could do was cry. Some days it was all I could do to put one foot in front of the other." But it kept her going, even when they received the call from Jamie saying her boyfriend had beaten her up, and through the two days following when they couldn't locate her.

Amazing what it takes to bring some prodigals home, isn't it? In Jamie's case it took a national disaster. Only a few weeks after terrorists attacked New York City's World Trade Center on September 11, 2001, she called her parents. Suddenly more than just her own personal world was falling apart. She wanted to come home.

"It will be two years in December," her mother writes. "God is working in her life, and we're so grateful. Now when I'm on the church platform and see her worshiping, it blesses me more than I can say. God continually shows us His grace!"

Yes, He does. And somehow He *gives* us grace as well, as we discovered the night of our own personal terrorist attack—a night that stays in my memory as both horrifying and pivotal.

It began with a raging phone fight between our son and his girlfriend. Afterward, he was incoherently angry and determined to go to see her. We wanted him to wait and calm down. This resulted in his again resisting our restraining efforts and rushing out into the night.

What transpired after that only he knows. Having long ago lost his driving privileges, he was on foot and claims to have been almost run down by a car. Evidently this was what frightened him into coming back home. But judging from how long he was gone, there must have been much more going on.

We knew, because we found evidence that he had been using drugs. Though we had never seen him strung out, it had become increasingly obvious that drugs were contributing to his escalating irrational behavior. Once or twice we broached the subject of treatment, but he always resisted, denying that there was a problem. Whether he had taken anything that night, we don't know.

Whatever happened, it brought him face-to-face with some personal demon. What my husband remembers is that he came bursting into the house, fell on the floor, and lay there curled into a fetal position. He was scared and crying, "I don't care where I go—just get me out of here!"

We spent most of the night calling one rehabilitation hospital after another only to be told that unless we had the right insurance—which we didn't—they couldn't help us. Jim finally found a treatment center two hours away in Reno, Nevada, that agreed to let us make payments. Just before dawn he loaded our son in the car and drove off.

It's hard to describe my feeling at that moment, standing in the doorway alone and shaken, yet relieved and hopeful that this might be the turning point we had been praying for.

For the next two weeks our only contact with our son was a couple of brief phone calls. It was during his third week of therapy that my mother died. Though the program didn't want to release him for the funeral, I wanted him there, thinking he might regret it later if he wasn't. Mostly though, this added personal loss left me aching to gather what remained of our family around me.

Two days afterward, he returned to Reno, checked himself out of the program, and moved in with his girlfriend. Later I discovered that she had threatened to drop him for someone else if he didn't come back and that the skinhead guy she dumped came over that same night with his gang and beat up everyone unlucky enough to be there.

Imagine our shock to also find out that our son and a buddy he had met in the program had been secretly doing drugs most of the time they were there. It took us three years to pay off his three-week "treatment," a bill amounting to $10,000.

Maybe it was worth the money to know that we did all we could. He had made his choice, and it was obviously time to stop trying to intervene. If only that meant we could stop living with the consequences. Unfortunately it doesn't work that way.

This time it was God who intervened on our behalf. Only a few weeks later, Jim received an unexpected phone call asking if he would consider taking a new pastoral assignment at a much larger church 300 miles away. It was a great opportunity, but we struggled with emotion over that decision. My still-grieving dad had no desire to deal with any more major upheaval, so he chose to move in with my brother and his family who lived about 75 miles away. I felt like a deserter. Our middle son wasn't about to move again. With little fight left in us, we reluctantly allowed him to stay behind with a family in the church in hopes he would finish high school. And, of course, it meant leaving the beloved church that had seen us through some of our darkest days.

It was not an easy parting, but in the end we felt God was closing a chapter and giving us an opportunity to start a new one. It also meant our oldest son would have to live with the decision he made without us there to bail him out. So with just our youngest son in tow, we made the move. Though we ended up staying there only two years, it gave us time to heal and assess the damage from a distance.

If only I could tell you we left all the pain behind! But with no spiritual resolution to our son's problems, we were—and still are—living with an open wound. That means that the pain at times continues to seep in around the edges of our lives. But with all chronic pain, you find ways to manage it. And so we've learned to continually give it to God.

Pastor's wife Jackie Klinsky summed it up like this: "The pain is ever present but keeps us on our knees."

Lord, You know better than anyone on earth the pain of living with the consequences of Your children's poor choices. How it must grieve You when the world rejects the love You offer, the eternal plan You've provided, and the incredible sacrifice You made to do it. Yet You continue to make available all that heaven has to offer. It's in that kind of love that we find hope and healing for our own pain. Continue to grant us patience and perseverance. In the name of Him whose grace is all sufficient. Amen.

What makes you hold on to a kid like that? Easy—we love him. I believe to fully understand the pain, you have to understand the love. Many well-meaning people over the years counseled us to pack our son's bags, put them on the doorstep, and not allow him to come back until he straightened out. Believe me—there were times it was tempting. I know in some cases it's the best and only viable alternative. But we never felt released to do it.

We may try to fool ourselves into thinking that if we can just stay angry with our children or disown them it won't hurt us as much. But I found it always hurts worse to be in denial and in the dark. We love our sons too much not to at least try to keep the doors of communication open. That has paid off many times over the years.

That doesn't mean, however, that we loved what they were doing. Many times we've had to ask God to help us look past their behavior and see them the way He sees us—warts, bruises, bumps, and all. The good news is that where there's love, there's hope. And we need all the hope we can get—especially when we're called upon to answer for our children's behavior by others in the community who are not so understanding.

6

Community Conflicts

Be wise in the way you act toward outsiders; make the most of every opportunity. Let your conversation be always full of grace, seasoned with salt, so that you may know how to answer everyone.
—Col. 4:5-6

It was a late summer night when Jonathan Boring walked with purpose toward Lakeshore Community Church. He had been making plans for days. Now the time had come. Kicking in the back door of the quiet, empty building, he entered a small Sunday School classroom, then began gathering papers and paint cans into a pile. Without the slightest hesitation, he placed a lighted cigarette inside a matchbook and dropped it onto the combustible heap. Just as he figured, it took about four minutes for the material to ignite. Whoof. The fire jumped to life, flames spreading in a fueled frenzy. Making a hasty retreat into the darkness, Jonathan had only one thought: *That'll show my dad and the world who's boss of my life.* Then the 15-year-old pastor's son went home and fell asleep.

It was later reported that the smoke and flames could be seen five miles away. Though perhaps not the global impact Jonathan had wished for, it certainly got the community's attention.

The next morning Jonathan's mother drove him to the scene, arriving just as fire crews finished their work. His dad was already there, along with the sheriff. "Let's go, Jon," the officer said. He never found out how they knew he did it. Maybe the fact he didn't deny it was proof enough. After being psychologically evaluated, he was incarcerated in juvenile hall. The conclusion? Jonathan wasn't crazy—just rebellious.

Meanwhile the community demonstrated so much bitterness toward him that Jonathan's parents felt they could no longer pastor there effectively. By the time he was released, they had purchased a gas station and a new home several miles away.

Though few experience a situation as dramatic as the Borings, parents of prodigals are bound to find themselves answering to certain segments of society for the deeds of their wayward children. What a stifling stigma this is for any minister! Here you are trying to be a light in the community while your child is determined to burn it up?

Naturally, a smaller setting allows for a more obvious negative impact. But even big communities can't provide parents of prodigals complete anonymity. It's a common conundrum. As rebellion escalates, behavior deteriorates along with regard for all authority. Tiny town or sprawling suburb, the shame is the same.

The first unpleasant encounters I recall during our boys' rebellious years were with teachers and school principals. These were small infractions at first—class disruptions, failure to comply with rules, poor learning performance, soon followed by skipping class, fighting, smoking, and profanity. It was so hard. Our sons were the ones breaking the rules; yet every time we were called in for a conference, I felt like the one being punished. These were things that went against everything we had tried to instill. We couldn't understand why our children were doing this; so how could we possibly explain their behavior to someone else? Yet I always felt obligated to try. Of course, we would make promises to correct them and make sure they did what they were supposed to. We were trying to be good parents and do the right thing for our children and all involved. But their defiance made us look like the ones coming up with a failing grade.

How well I remember the first time a policeman came to our door, his late-night knock waking us to a disoriented scramble for robes and slippers. My first fear was that one of the boys had been in an accident. Turns out that it did involve reckless driving. "Your son and a carload of friends were weaving in and out of traffic," I heard him tell my husband, "pretending to shoot at other cars with a toy pistol." Amazing how quickly your emotions can turn. For a brief moment I was the one who wanted to shoot someone. Fortunately, my son was still sitting in the police car.

Sadly, the community service people have no reason to understand. They don't know your child, circumstances, family heritage, or spiritual convictions. Most times it doesn't matter. They're doing their jobs and simply view your child as any other punk perpetrator. "But it's not the way it seems!" we want to shout. "This is not the child we raised! We're pastors, you see, ministers of the gospel, and . . ." And what? Sure, we know the endearing qualities of our children, but the judicial system and community know the awful things the child has done. It's hard to argue with the facts. All we can do is try to be cooperative and let our own character be above reproof.

To this extent I did learn to be thankful. There were a number of times the police and others prevented our children from getting into more serious trouble. Punitive priorities notwithstanding, we did often encounter compassion and leniency toward providing second chances. Occasionally we even encountered humor.

One night my husband received a call from a police officer asking him to come pick up our middle son, who had broken curfew. Our oldest son, decked out in black leather jacket, boots, and punk hairstyle, decided to go along for the ride. Observing his get-up, the officer couldn't resist inquiring why he was dressed that way.

"I'm on the side of the working man," he answered sarcastically.

"Oh. So you're working."

Taken off guard, he answered defensively, "No."

"Well," replied the officer, sharing a smile with my husband. "If you really want to represent the working man, you might think about getting a job."

It was that kind of ridiculous rationale that made us not want to answer for this kid anymore. *He wants to make his own decisions,* we reasoned, *so let him answer for himself.* The legal reality, however, is that while children are minors, we're responsible to the community for them whether we want to be or not.

It's when they come of age that we face a different dilemma. I'll never forget the first phone call, years into our son's adulthood, telling us he was in jail.

"It's all a big mistake," he convinced us. So we bailed him out.

I thought it was the worst morning of my life, but I was wrong. The second time he was jailed on the same offense was worse—because I knew we couldn't conscientiously bail him out again. When his angry disconnect finally stopped echoing in my heart, the questions started. *Did we do the right thing? How long would he have to be there? What would happen to him?* This time the courts would decide without seeking our involvement. Now there was no one to whom we must answer but ourselves. I still don't know which was harder.

While there's no debate about our responsibility to answer for our children on a community level, our interaction there is (hopefully) sporadic and short-lived. Our place of ministry is a different matter. These are the people we must face on a regular basis. When it becomes apparent that our children's errors in judgment or downright defiance cannot escape our church's attention, so many things go through our minds. Will the church hold us responsible? Will they still consider us credible to counsel? Reeling with our own sense of failure, we no longer consider ourselves worthy to set an example for others. Not knowing how people will react, we live with fear of embarrassment in the event they request our resignation. Our moral and spiritual obligations weigh heavily. Surely there is no place a pastor feels greater conflict.

After church one Sunday night, my husband went with a group to a nearby coffee shop. I had gone home exhausted, anticipating how early my alarm clock would ring the next morning. But that wasn't all. What few people knew was that our oldest son had been missing for three days.

It was toward the end of the evening as everyone was preparing to leave that Jim looked up to see our transient son walk through the front door. Needless to say, it was an uncomfortable moment. Not wanting to extend his embarrassment, those in the group quickly mumbled their good-byes and left. But any humiliation my husband felt quickly evaporated. The boy looked like walking death. Half-starved and strung out, he had been living in someone's car. My husband embraced him, bought him something to eat, and convinced him to come home and get some sleep.

In an article written for *Leadership* magazine entitled "Pastoring with Hurts at Home"[1] a friend describes his personal pastoral dilemma. He writes of meeting his 19-year-old son for lunch, hoping it would provide an opportunity to dissuade his plans to marry, a topic already much-debated by the family because of his age and unfinished education.

Their salads had just arrived when his son spoke words he was in no way prepared for. "Dad, we're going to have a baby. I'm sorry to hurt you, but we need to get married right away."

Picking through the rest of his meal while grasping for some reasonable response, all the pastor could think was *Now there's no way to keep the church from knowing. And I'll be called to account.*

Then came another realization. The bulletin with his Sunday sermon title, the first in a series entitled "The Future Family," was on its way to press. Somehow he had to stop it.

Talk about church conflict. Yet repeatedly I've observed that when a church loves its pastor, it will rise to the occasion in amazing ways. When the pastor in the above story presented his family situation to the board and offered his resignation, they refused.

"To a person," he writes, "the board affirmed me and my family. One reminded me of how I had stood with him in a similar crisis. We prayed and cried together."

Not only were there no confrontations or accusations from the church family—some even helped with medical expenses. Others threw a baby shower.

Another pastor's wife relates a similar scenario. In an attempt to set a tough-love example for their church, her husband had taken a hard stand against their rebellious son, showing little personal emotion. One Sunday night, following a particularly volatile family confrontation, the mother decided to stay home from church. The thought of facing people was unbearable. Her stoic husband went, but no sooner had he stepped to the pulpit than he broke down into sobs. Without hesitation, the congregation gathered around him in a time of prayer and healing. Not only did this unify the church, but it soon led to reconciliation with his son.

My friend Sue Patterson tells how over an extended period of time a team of intercessors from their church organized drive-by prayer sessions past their prodigal son's house. Though he never knew, Sue credits this committed act of love for turning the tide in his life.

I wonder if it could be that we in ministry are so accustomed to filling the role of one who gives counsel and comfort that we can't imagine being on the receiving end, or that by hiding our personal pain we rob our congregations of the real-life opportunity to put into practice what we've preached. Then it's up to the individual church to decide how willing it is to step up to the prodigal plate.

In our case, the church hit a home run.

Of course, as long as our boys were at home, we insisted that they attend church. They weren't always excited about it, but they complied. They would even at times invite friends, mostly so they could split right afterward. While we had some control over how our kids came dressed for church, we couldn't change their friends' attire. In those days the most common outward display of rebellion was spiked, fluorescent hair and lots of leather. Can you imagine the pew-full of interesting dress and hairstyles this provided? I have to hand it to our church. Most made a point to accept and reach out to these kids—or at least keep the stares to a minimum. Especially for some of the older folks, this surely meant reaching way beyond their own comfort zone.

It so happened during this time that one of our sons' best friends was tragically killed in an automobile accident. No need to say what a devastating impact this had on our sons and their friends. Not coincidentally, our youth pastor had an already-planned special service on the schedule for the week following the accident dealing with what happens after death. Seventeen of our sons' friends came to church that night and heard God's plan of salvation.

Yes, we're called upon to answer to the community, Christian and otherwise, for our children's poor choices. But it also provides us incredible opportunities to reach those we might not have otherwise come in contact with. For that I have no regrets.

It would be less than honest, though, to say we didn't experience tinges of regret when observing other ministers' children who did not rebel, who by all outward appearance seemed to be doing well and making their parents proud. I just couldn't help but feel a sort of envy at times. I was never really bitter, mind you, just wistful for what might have been and sad for what we were missing. OK—and some occasional self-pity. There were times we felt out of place in ministerial settings, as if we bore a brand on our foreheads or were standing outside some invisible circle. Not that anyone ever intentionally made us feel that way or even expected us to answer for our sons, but I'm sure there were silent speculations about what had happened to fracture our family.

One particular incident comes to mind regarding a ministry couple with whom we frequently had fellowship. They had grown up in another culture, and English was their second language. They had a boy the same age as our middle son who was clean-cut, nicely dressed, and respectful. Our son wore long hair and grubby garb, and his surliness was as hard to miss as a mustard stain on his shirtsleeve. Obviously there was more than just a cultural difference.

One night we dropped the boys off at a video arcade. As we started to leave, the mother rolled down the car window and spoke seriously to her son in their native language. I didn't need an interpretation to sense her concern, but she must have felt politely obligated. "I just told him not to do anything he wasn't comfortable with." I knew she had every right and reason to instruct her child; still I was hurt beyond explanation.

Truth is, years before facing the challenges with our own children, my husband had some experience with community conflict by observing his pastor-parents' struggle with his older brother. Whether it was growing up in a small southern Illinois town that provided little in the way of entertainment or the fact their parents had to work full time supporting themselves and the ministry that caused their problems, no one knows. Something proved to be a bad combination for Jim's brother, Dwaine. Bright and energetic, by age 16 he had become the ringleader for a group of local mischief-makers. It was when the mischief turned to malice that the real trouble began.

Jim jokes now that his most nostalgic memories of growing up include cleaning the "clinkers" out of an old coal stove, hunting for rabbits, playing sports, and the police knocking on their front door. The sad truth was that it reached the point that any local trouble automatically brought the police to their house looking for Dwaine.

Within three years his brother had been kicked out of two high schools with no hope of reenrolling. The family tried moving to another nearby town, but even then he barely managed to stay ahead of trouble. Many nights Jim remembers coming home and hearing his parents in their bedroom praying for Dwaine. Those prayers were soon answered. In the end a community conflict served as one small turning point.

Dwaine had a wonderful voice and, reputation notwithstanding, was often asked to sing for church. Stepping onto the platform one night, he dropped his sheet music. Bending down to pick it up, a pack of cigarettes fell out of his shirt pocket onto the altar. It's one thing to light up in the dark; quite another to have your dark double life lit up in public. This delinquent was definitely disconcerted.

Not long afterward, Dwaine voluntarily laid his cigarettes along with his whole heart on the altar, surrendering the rest of his life to serving God. He not only finished his education but also graduated with honors, going on eventually to earn a doctorate. He recently just retired after more than 40 years of ministry that included 25 years teaching in a prestigious Bible college.

It occurs to me that this story may raise a question with which some of us have guiltily grappled: is there something hereditary about being a prodigal? I'll leave to the psychologists and theologians the debate about what's passed on through generation to generation. All I know is this: there's no denying that we all inherit a sinful nature. But our real heritage, according to Scripture, is to be a child of God. Paul tells us, "The Spirit himself testifies with our spirit that we are God's children. Now if we are children, then we are heirs—heirs of God and coheirs with Christ, if indeed we share in his sufferings in order that we may also share in his glory" (Rom. 8:16-17). That, friends, is the heritage we must never stop claiming for our children.

There's no question about it—having to answer to the community, the church, and our own peers for the negative decisions and actions of our children can be hurtful and humiliating, perhaps more so because it means having to come up with answers for ourselves or discovering that you have no answers, something not all pastors see as a positive.

Once after a particularly upsetting phone conversation regarding our son, I called Jim. No sooner had I shared the details than he launched into preacher mode, trying his best to offer some solution. "Honey," I interrupted. "I don't need you to tell me what to do right now. I just need you to listen."

We don't have to know all the answers to encourage someone else. So many are ashamed to admit what's going on with their children, and they feel alone and are perhaps even afraid to love their children, because they're so far out there. We can offer them a ray of hope just by listening. The best listeners, after all, are those who don't just sympathize but empathize out of their own experience.

Here, too, is a way of turning our pain into positive action by offering it back to the community. How well I remember sitting in a circle of parents who had come for an orientation at one of the alternative schools our son attended. Mind you, most kids end up in alternative schools for a reason. It didn't take long to hear some sad stories and see some hopeless faces. I can't imagine dealing with a rebellious child without the Lord's help. Want to double the size of your church? Offer a support group for parents of wayward kids.

Our experiences with our children have taken us places we would have never gone and introduced us to people we would have never otherwise met. We've been given insight into lifestyles that many ministers never see. As a result, I've lost most fear of weird-looking kids. When I see them in the mall or on the street, hanging out, looking so tough and troubled, I often want to hug them. They're someone's prodigals.

If you think that would take more courage than you have, let me tell you something: it takes courage to be the parent of a prodigal. You may not feel all that brave. But if you're hanging in there, keeping faith, and sharing hope, then you, my cowardly lion friend, have courage. You have the courage not just to answer your community but the courage to touch it as well.

I know. None of us wanted to be that kind of hero. *I have begun a journey,* a small entry in my journal reads, *not as a result of being launched but more of being capsized and set adrift.* It's amazing when you're set adrift how those survival instincts kick in. How much of what you've learned are you willing to share with others? In the end, it may be the difference between surviving and thriving.

It was these very qualities in the lives of Jonathan Boring's parents that gave his story a happy ending. He wouldn't know for years that he was released from juvenile hall only because his dad pled with the court for custody. The judge was amazed that the father would even consider taking back a son who had visibly destroyed all he had worked for.

For the next two years Jonathan went to school, worked in the gas station, and stayed out of major trouble. But since his attitude had changed little, his father's attempts to restrict him caused them to be in almost constant disagreement. Not far into his senior year, Jonathan dropped out of high school to go on the road with a traveling rock band. It would prove to be a long and winding road involving drugs, sex, and hard partying.

All along the way, though, his mother's faithful letters full of love and encouragement somehow always found him. It was through that open door of communication that, following a stint in the Air Force and a painful failed marriage, Jonathan finally returned home. Broken in health and in spirit, he was amazed but thankful to be welcomed again by his parents.

Not long afterward, he stood alone one day with God on the side of a nearby mountain, pouring out all his prodigal pain. "I sobbed out a confession that came from the deepest, most hidden part of my soul," says Jonathan. "I told the Lord how sorry I was for my life and that I wanted to know Him like my dad did." Always faithful, God sent a customized compliance.

Today, no longer in conflict with God or his parents, Jonathan Boring serves as a pastor. And guess where—in one of the same small communities where his father once served.

Lord, we need wisdom to know how to deal with those to whom we must answer for our children's behavior. Help us to see even these hurtful, humiliating experiences as opportunities for ministry. May we somehow lay aside our own pride for the sake of our children and be, in the process, not only better parents but better pastors and brighter lights in our communities. In Jesus' name we pray. Amen.

So many things revolve around our prodigal children that come down to sorting through the fine-line issues of dignity, self-respect, and pride. "We don't have to worry about losing our dignity," my husband Jim once remarked ruefully. "We have none left to lose." But you know what we found surprising about reaching that point? It can be freeing.

At some point we have to lay aside the pain and humiliation in favor of pursuing what's best for our families. That means we stop worrying so much about what others think and begin seeking instead only what Christ requires in every situation.

Most often that means starting at home.

7

Home Is Where the Hurt Is

*In him you too are being built together to become
a dwelling in which God lives by his Spirit.*
—Eph. 2:22

"Look at the birch trees—they must be 25 feet tall."

Jim nodded. "But the house looks the same, just smaller than I remember."

We sat in our rental car, staring at the square, flat-roofed house in Anchorage, Alaska, that had once been our home. An early-fall conference had lured us back, and we couldn't resist a quick visit to the old neighborhood. I had loved that house, our very first, brand-new when we moved in. I was surprised by how ordinary it looked now, even a little sad and run-down. *But then it's Alaska,* I reminded myself. *Twenty-five years of winters have taken their toll.*

Twenty-five years. Had it really been that long since those fledgling years of ministry? Another glance at the trees told me it was true. They had been saplings when we planted them alongside a huge driftwood log surrounded by native wildflowers. Three trees, all grown up—just like our three boys.

The years had taken a toll there, too.

Ironic how the coldest places on earth can hold the warmest memories. And vice versa. It was only five years after we left Alaska that our sunny California home weathered the cold front of confusion rivaling any Arctic climate. There we trudged knee-deep through some of our most chilling seasons. Driving by that house still produces an emotional shiver; the memories are like frostbite.

With our oldest son determined to defy our authority and take control over his own life, our home was soon in almost constant turmoil. Despite our best peacekeeping efforts, the initial testing ground had become a seismic battleground, rumbling with underlying issues. Now every effort to direct or discipline became a gauntlet with control as the grand guerdon, the coveted prize. Why couldn't he see that the choices he was making were potentially self-destructive? Our attempts to intervene only resulted in angry confrontations. The more the battle escalated, one thing became clear. It didn't matter who came out on top—nobody would win.

Of course, the last thing we wanted was for our church to know how bad things were at home; so we tried our best to hold it all together. Soon it was tearing us all apart.

Home. Happy or hurting, warm climate or cold, it's the stage where real-life dramas play out. But unlike the movies and television, we don't get scripts. Nor are our dilemmas solved at the end of a half-hour episode. Of course, we trust God to be our prompter, try to follow His divine direction, then expect happy endings. But the daily dialogue is ours to improvise as we go along.

Truth is, as pain assumes a prominent role in the parsonage, our best performances are often given at church. Some of us should be up for Academy Awards. And most amazing, it requires only a single prop: a mask with a well-crafted smile. I've often thought the glove compartment of every clergy car should come equipped with smiles, standard issue, one for each member of the family. Then you could just slip one on before stepping out of the car and into the sanctuary. So convenient for the tiff that doesn't get resolved in time for morning worship.

Should we feel guilty? After all, it's neither appropriate nor acceptable for those in ministry to stand before the congregation and shake out every piece of dirty laundry. Thank goodness for our homes. They provide a safe place to knead out life's little lumps away from public scrutiny. I dare say no shepherd's cottage is perpetually peaceful. There are times it just wouldn't do to have the sheep wandering in unbidden. That would be baaad news.

But a prodigal's performance is a very different kind of drama. It doesn't just bring down the curtain—it jeopardizes the whole playhouse. When the parsonage doors are broken, splintered from the inside, the entire family is left exposed to the critics.

How is it that the worst-case scenarios with pastors' children always seem to erupt on Saturday night? My husband and I have pondered that point more than once. It happens too often to be a coincidence. Then we had no choice but to drag ourselves to church the next morning. Sleep deprived and heavy-hearted, we sometimes didn't even notice—or care—when the smiley mask fell off.

It's a scene replayed on many parsonage platforms.

"We received the phone call at 4:30 in the morning," writes one pastor. "It was the police. Our son had been arrested for grand theft larceny. *What could this mean?* I thought. *Not my son.* Only after I hung up the phone did I realize it was Sunday and that I had to preach three times that morning. Then all I could think was *Where did I go wrong?* and *Can our marriage take any more?*

In other words, will the church or our home survive this? Good question.

It's the simple nature of families that when one struggles, all are affected. Under normal conditions, that can be a good thing. When a member is working toward a positive goal or experiences an unexpected turn of events, family provides a ready-made, unified support system. As author R. A. Scott puts it, "Familyhood supplies irreplaceable assets."

True. But let that member exhibit a sudden, negative change of behavior or direction, and it can have the opposite effect. The family is left confused and divided on what the appropriate response or necessary intervention should be. Then it's inevitable that tension turns inward.

In the case of difficult or defiant children, marriages become strained as husbands and wives disagree on the appropriate action or disciplinary measures. Dissimilar ways of handling the stress can result in a communication chasm. Siblings are torn in their loyalties and left grieving the loss of a once-close brother or sister who is now absent or a stranger. Well-meaning (or not) family members offer unsolicited advice that only adds to the emotional turmoil. In some cases, the burden is compounded by other extenuating, exhausting circumstances such as illness or the responsibility of caring for other dependent family members.

Pastor Roger and Norma Womack's story (not their real names) serves to illustrate these elements well. Their son, Daniel, had been dating a girl named Linda. Though both families were Christians, it didn't take the Womacks long to figure out that the young couple had become sexually involved. Other family members were whispering about it, too. However, Linda's folks had blinders on and refused to accept the truth. "Not our daughter!"

So they invited trouble by allowing the kids to be alone in their home. Regarding the Womacks as rigid and restrictive, Linda's mother even resorted to planning outings that conflicted with Daniel's family celebrations, forcing him to choose between the two. Naturally, he gravitated toward his girlfriend's family.

Other circumstances fueled the hurt. Roger Womack had not entered the ministry until late in life. Growing up in a non-Christian home, he had experienced many difficult circumstances. Though these had eventually led to his salvation and ultimate call to ministry, Daniel was the product of a marriage that had ended in divorce several years prior. Granted, he was still young when his dad remarried, but the birth of a half-brother soon after only seemed to add to the confusion. Not many years later came another challenge. His stepmother was diagnosed with multiple sclerosis, leaving her dependent and extremely angry with God.

"I can't imagine that I was pleasant to my family during that devastating time of adjustment," Norma admits.

Enter the lustful teenage romance. The already crumbling walls began to tumble rapidly.

"My husband expressed a lot of anger toward Daniel during that time," Norma continues, "probably because when he was a child, his own parents never expressed love toward him. He was stretched too thin between the church, a sick wife, a teenager, and our younger son."

The final blow-up came—as is often typical—not over the sexual relationship but because Daniel decided to pierce his ear. The ultimatum was given: Get rid of the earring or move out.

Daniel packed his bags.

Shortly afterward, Daniel and Linda broke up; but by that time the damage was done. Filled with conflict, ignoring what his heart told him was right, Daniel continued to pursue a lifestyle involving alcohol, drugs, and sex—a lifestyle that was hurtful to his parents, to himself, and to God.

"The whole situation was very hard on our family," says Norma. "His brother missed him at home. He made short visits, but they left our younger son distraught, because he knew Daniel had been drinking and using tobacco."

"And we were both angry at my husband for telling him to leave. Poor Roger. He felt like a failure as a pastor and a parent.

The stress level in our home was pretty high during this time."

No doubt.

What do we do when the place that should be a safe haven begins posting severe storm warnings? Some of us run around, sandbagging like crazy. Others face the fury head-on in hopes of eventually finding the eye of calm.

For us, these were churning and uncharted waters. Soon we were caught in a swirl of anger, fear, and worry. Would giving in to one thing open the door to more difficult decisions, decisions we might not be prepared to make, resulting in consequences that affected not only our son but the entire family? No wonder it felt as if our home might be sucked up and spiraled away at any moment.

How can children possibly understand that sometimes parents react as strongly out of fear as they do anger? I'll admit it—we weren't always wise in picking battles with our children. Early on the prodigal path the usual conflagrations flared over clothes, music, choices of friends, and places to go. *Just part of normal teenage rebellion,* we figured. *It always takes a few head-butts to reach a meeting of the minds.*

Following a mad rush out the door one Sunday morning, we were halfway to church before I noticed what my middle son was wearing—old, torn jeans, a wrinkled shirt, and untied tennis shoes. Not appropriate attire in my opinion, and I let him know it. The clothes clash raged for a few minutes; then, in all seriousness, he turned to me.

"Mom, do you really think God cares what I wear to church?"

As my mouth was open, ready to reply, the impact of his statement reduced me to silence. No doubt God was just glad he was there. And I should be, too.

End of debate.

All parents experience some hurt and rejection when their children refuse advice or fail to appreciate their efforts. But for pastor-parents there's another dynamic. We're ministry models, the ones who counsel others. What does it say to our congregations when our own children reject that counsel? We can't help but fret over that.

Like most parents, we were convinced that if we kept a tight rein, we could turn the buggy. When the contest for the reins sent the buggy into a slide, we knew we were on a collision course.

The first major challenge came when our then-14-year-old son wanted to get his ear pierced. (What is it with the earring issue? Keep in mind, though, that this was the early 1980s.)

His dad and I drew a line in the sand. "Absolutely not." There would be no debate on this issue.

"Why not?"

We drew out the big guns. "Because we're your parents, and we said so."

That strategy really worked. Out he went that very night and asked one of his friends to pierce his ear.

Like any miffed mom, I responded in rational fashion: I hauled him to our family doctor for a tetanus shot—and hoped it hurt.

Looking back, I wonder, *So what exactly was the issue there?* If foresight could have told me that was the worst thing he would ever do, would our response have been different? Of course.

But we didn't. And it wasn't. It was only the first scrimmage in what became a long war of wills.

The more we determined to hold our "because-we're-the-parents" stance, the more complex things became. Was there a direct correlation between the pierced-ear incident and anything that happened later? I'm not sure. Still, you can't help wishing you had handled it—and a hundred subsequent things—better.

Of course, these small conflicts were just symptoms of a more dangerous disease. The interests our son was embracing at that time symbolized a lifestyle we tried to steer him away from. Fueled by support from his new "friends," long-buried feelings exploded, leaving sinkholes on the home turf. With our domicile continually under construction and caution flags popping up everywhere, we pored over the biblical blueprints.

Meanwhile, our younger children watched to see what we would do.

When the home fires heat up, the smoke of uncertainty blurs everyone's perspective. Perhaps no one gets caught in the middle more than siblings. Like Daniel's brother, they can't help but be affected by the way their brother or sister behaves—and how their parents react. *What,* they wonder, *is my role in this developing drama? Should I take sides? And if so, whose?* Some just choose to stay out of it.

One of the most difficult dilemmas parents dealing with a

prodigal face is knowing how to help other children in the family understand what's happening. Yet the worst thing we can do is not address it. Everything during our prodigal parenting years seemed to revolve around our oldest son. We never intended to exclude or neglect the other children; yet his behavior could not be ignored. It demanded our attention and often monopolized our time. No wonder other kids in the family develop their own behavioral problems. It's a way of getting attention, even if it's negative.

It's hard, too, to avoid making comparisons. If you have a child who's doing well, it's always tempting to say, "Why can't you be more like your brother or sister?" Even if you don't say it, you may unconsciously display it by treating him or her differently.

Of course, no kid is ever going to feel that he or she has been treated fairly all the time. You can drive yourself crazy trying to make everything come out equal. How many times over the years I heard, "That's not fair!" My favorite response to that predictable protest was the phrase uttered by countless parents, "Sorry, but nobody ever said life would be fair." Soon my boys became programmed to the point at which no sooner had I said, "Sorry, but . . ." than they would just roll their eyes and say, "We know—we know."

I suppose at some point you have to ask yourself what causes some children to create such chaos. As we mentioned, personality plays a definite part. It's the only explanation why children who grow up in the same home environment react so differently. Even their memories of the same exact event can vary drastically. Understanding and accepting the differences in personalities goes a long way toward applying fair treatment.

The difference in our three boys' personalities was glaring from the get-go. Before he could walk, our oldest son displayed an obvious need for security and instant gratification. As soon as he was awake, he wanted someone to get him out of his crib, to know we were there. If we didn't respond immediately, he would stand up and bang the crib against the wall. It was his way of saying, "I'm awake. Now everybody up!" When this kid wanted attention, he wanted it *now* and would find the quickest, loudest way of getting it. We've often said that he's been banging up against one wall or another ever since. No doubt, that need for security and control played a part in other impetuous choices and dependencies later on.

Our middle son is the observing, analytical one. He soon discovered that if he threw his bottle onto the floor, someone would come in and give it back and then try to get him to drink it. There was just always something more fascinating going on around him, and he didn't want to miss anything. Twisting and turning to see, he could hardly pay attention long enough to finish the bottle. He's proven very good at observing and analyzing his way through life. Questioning everything, it's evident he's bent on making decisions in his own time and on his own terms. And it's still sometimes hard to get his attention.

Our youngest son was bright-eyed and easygoing. If we had left him in his crib all day, you could almost be sure he would find ways to entertain himself. But even good-natured children can take things to extremes. At the first preschool conference, his teacher commented on how it wasn't unusual for him to just jump up in the middle of quiet time and do a little dance. Concerned over such disruptive behavior, I asked, "Do you think he's craving attention or needs more discipline?" She stifled a smile. "No. I'm sure he just feels like it." There were a number of things he did later just because he felt like it that came close to getting him into much more serious trouble.

Nothing sums up the difference in our boys' personalities like their Mother's Day card when they were about 15, 13, and 10, which, judging from the flowery front, their dad picked out. Oldest son wrote, *Happy Mom's Day! Things are getting better. Thanks for putting up with me.* Middle, also possessing an obvious literary flair, wrote, *Mom, it would be foolish to try to put into words how much I love and appreciate you. I hope that instead, my actions will be able to emulate what I'm sure you already know.* And laid-back number three wrote, *Happy Mother's Day! Have a nice one day off. Ha! Ha!*

As if that would ever happen.

Individual personalities require different dealings and discipline. What works with one child simply won't with another. So what do you do when nothing works at all? Over the years, we gathered gallons of advice. "Be firm." "Lay down the law." "Take away their privileges." "Don't let them get away with that." And later: "Pack his bags and put them on the doorstep." "Change the locks."

We tried most of them many times. Some failed. Others worked

—at least temporarily. But there were dynamics that people who've never had to deal with a defiant child—the ones most likely to offer advice—can never possibly understand. These were the ones who, seeing no obvious improvement, would just shake their critical heads. I could almost hear them thinking, *Poor, pathetic pastor and wife. They just don't get it. If they'd just do it right, it would work.*

Excuse me! I wanted to shout. *We got it—we tried it! It didn't work! But thanks for adding to our pressure!* Of course, those words were never actually uttered; that would have been unpastorly.

It's going to happen as people in the church begin to see and hear what's going on. I know people gave advice out of concern for us as much as our children. Unfortunately, some don't always get the facts straight. Nor is it necessary, even for the sake of accuracy, that everyone knows everything. It's not going to help our child to be embarrassed or feel that we've shared their problems with the entire church community. And, sad to add, there are those with less-than-divine motives for wanting all the dirt. We soon learned to sift the words of wisdom sacredly and soulfully, then follow only what was God-directed and what we felt our family could live with.

I'm thankful for a few special and trusted friends who came alongside, always seeming to be there at the exact time we needed them, like my dear friend Catherine, who believed in my boys and never failed to point out the positives; or our wonderful youth pastors John and Jacqueline, who brought (and continue to bring) unconditional love, hope, and humor into all our lives; and uniquely gifted minister friends like Donnie Moore and Scott Sinner, who purposely pursued our prodigals—across a parking lot and a camp ground, in two different cases.

These are the kind of people we all need in our lives to provide hope in the form of an objective viewpoint, people who care enough to preach, pray, and encourage, whether they know all the details or not. They'll be the ones to share not just in your pain but also in your celebration. May you be so blessed.

It helps, too, in the search for identity if children have a sense of family history and heritage. One summer just as the situation at home began to deteriorate, Jim and I decided to take a vacation back to the Midwest by car. Though we had often visited grandparents, they were usually limited fly-ins with little time to take in the surrounding scenery. Just once we wanted to peruse with our boys all the places where we grew up. Though we figured they would be bored to death, we were pleasantly surprised. Each familiar landmark seemed to spawn a story, giving them not only vitals but also visuals of what it was like for us, growing up in a different time and place. And, of course, they met all the wacky and wonderful relatives.

The change of scenery was good for all of us, painting a larger landscape of who we were as a family. It proved to be a priceless opportunity, especially since it was only two years later that my mom entered the nursing home and Dad came to live with us.

Admittedly, it was difficult having my dad's added set of emotional needs to meet. But since he spent most of his day at the nursing home with my mother, I had a reprieve, and he was spared much of the conflict. The thing I didn't realize until later was how it gave my boys a chance to observe my relationship with my own parents and their relationship to each other. There's no doubt that watching Dad's devotion to my mother and hearing his stories made for a deeper family dynamic, something my children have definitely reflected on as they mature and see us getting older.

It's true that grandparents and other close family members don't always fully comprehend what all the fuss is about or make positive contributions. "These kids never had to face a depression and world war, for goodness' sake." Their unsolicited or untimely advice may even add to the tension. Still, I believe it helps children to know that there are people other than parents who care about them, even if they don't always know how to show it. And some prodigals will listen to other family members when they'll toss aside their parents' words like candy wrappers. In the end, having Dad live with us definitely proved much more a blessing than a burden.

Tough as the home turf gets, there's something to be said for keeping your children there as long as possible, at least while they're young. Why? Because even as we weave through the workings, we can still be offering direction, attempting to reason, setting forth spiritual guidelines and modeling values. According to a well-known saying, lessons are more caught than taught. As more time passes, I realize that my children remember and absorbed much more than it seemed at the time. Once they leave home, that influence is drastically diminished.

Also, it gives you more time to build traditions and memories. These are things that hopefully they'll miss enough somewhere down the prodigal path to be drawn back. I have to believe the biblical prodigal sitting in that pigpen must have mentally maneuvered every familiar room in his father's house more than once—and dreamed at night about sleeping in his own bed. We know for certain that he thought about food. Every family has their favorite special meals. If there's anything that will bring our boys running from the distant land, it's biscuits and gravy for breakfast or the traditional Braddy birthday lasagna.

We also have our favorite family videos and music, plus certain stories we love to retell when we're together. It's amazing how even some of the worst disaster stories eventually soften around the edges, even become funny.

Home—even one with some painful memories—is still the place you hang your heart.

In all honesty, there were times Jim and I were the ones who wanted to run away from home. Once, in the aftermath of yet another horrific family feud, my husband blurted, "Maybe we should just go back to Alaska!" Caught off guard, I could only blink. Then we both burst out laughing. It wasn't even—pardon the pun—a remote option, but it made for great comic relief. To this day, when any kind of frustration boils over, it's still our little private joke.

For us, Alaska still symbolizes that place of peace and quiet, far removed not just logistically but also emotionally. Those were the early, less complicated years of our marriage, ministry, and family, the innocent years when our kids were, well—just kids. No wonder seeing that house with the now-tall birches brought back so many memories.

When I speak of the time we spent in Alaska, people always ask how we liked it. How did we stand the months of dark and cold? We loved it. Yes, there were some weary winters. But Alaska also has amazing summers that more than compensate—long hours of daylight that produce an unusual clarity of color and incredible growth. Not a bad thing to remember when the cold, dark days settle over our homes.

Let me remind you that as we remain faithful, God promises to compensate us. "I will repay you for the years the locust has eaten," He promises the Israelites in Joel 2:25—a promise I believe we can personally appropriate. If you're looking for a book of encouragement along those lines, it's a theme my friend Jan Coleman eloquently elaborates in her book *After the Locusts: Restoring Ruined Dreams, Reclaiming Wasted Years.* Following a painful failed marriage, Jan also made the prodigal pilgrimage with her daughter, Amy, who experimented with everything from dope to devil worship. It took seven years for her to turn around, but Amy knew that no matter what she had done, her mother loved her. Today they're best friends.

I packed many lessons when we left Alaska. The night our front porch blew off in a winter storm serves to illustrate just three. First, you have to hold tight when everything around you is changing. Second, when things get rough, you find you can get along without a lot of things you previously thought were necessary. And third, you can always rebuild if you have a good foundation.

And my all-time favorite Alaskan adage: No matter how long or harsh the winter, spring never fails to come. It's because of God's faithfulness through every storm and season that our children and grandchildren still have a place to call home.

Lord, the words on our old family plaque read, "Christ is the Head of this house, the unseen Host at every meal, the silent Listener to every conversation." Let it be so. Whether our homes are happy or hurting, be present. Use every circumstance to build us together, that we may become a dwelling in which Your Spirit lives. In Jesus' name we pray. Amen

When we left Alaska, our congregation presented us with some beautiful gold nugget jewelry. It was hard to believe those shiny nuggets had only recently come out of a mine belonging to a member of our congregation. Obviously they were gems well worth digging out, polishing, and cherishing, something it may help to remember when the family God wants you to be gets temporarily lost in the rubble.

8

Those Whom God Has Joined

What God has joined together, let man not separate.
—Mark 10:9

I stood in front of the bedroom closet jerking clothes haphazardly off their hangers and tossing them into a suitcase on the bed. Following too many tension-filled months of frustration, the anger and weariness had erupted big time. It seemed almost every discussion now between Jim and me ended with mutual faultfinding and finger-pointing. The most recurrent disagreement concerned the best way to discipline our children, particularly our oldest son.

I had come to despise my role as the disciplinarian. "Let's just give him one more chance," Jim would say. But I always ran out of patience before our son ran out of chances.

I had had it with feeling like the bad guy.

"What are you doing?" Jim asked, trying to keep a level tone.

"Leaving." I blindly grabbed a few more clothes, hangers and all.

A short silence, then "Where are you planning to go?"

Mid-jerk, I stopped. I hadn't thought about that. My parents no longer had a home. My brother had his own family and responsibilities. And I certainly didn't want anyone in the church to know. My friend Catherine? No. Only a temporary solution at best.

Like ice water in my face, the truth hit me. I was stuck.

If pastors have a theme scripture, it must be Gal. 6:9—"Let us not become weary in doing good, for at the proper time we will reap a harvest if we do not give up." I understand what Paul is saying here. Don't slack off. Keep going. There's a lot to do and much to be gained if you hold out to the end. And I wholeheartedly agree. But when you're fighting a constant battle at home, this business of doing good can wear you to a frazzle. No wonder you end up turning the guns on each other.

Jim was doing his best to cast vision and meet the needs of our growing church. But with everything else that was transpiring, the routine of running even a small church had taken on gigantic proportions. To help make ends meet, I had taken an outside job, a high-stress position with an employment company that sometimes required working long hours. It's not that we were weary in doing good; we were just plain weary—and tired of fighting our kids.

Still, we carried on. In all honesty, though, I felt like the one stretched thinnest, trying to give 100-percent to the church, my family, and my job. Convinced that I was doing my best under the circumstances, in reality I was running near empty. Hadn't a mechanic cautioned me one time about letting my car get too low on fuel? "Then all the sludge that settles in the bottom of the tank gets drawn into the engine." That was my problem. I was sucked dry and running on soul sludge.

On top of everything else, I now found myself part of the sandwich generation—those caught between caring for their aging parents and caring for their own families. *Sandwich generation? How about rubber-band generation? Surely I'm not the only one being stretched to hold it all together.* Just when my children no longer seemed to want my help and advice, my parents needed it. What irony! How had life taken such a drastic change in such a short time?

Now not only were my nerves frayed, but our marriage was starting to unravel as well.

I'm still not sure why I didn't quit the job to stay home and care for my mother. We probably could have tightened our belts and gotten by financially. Once my distressed dad even offered to pay us what the nursing home was charging. My brother repeatedly reassured me that, due to Mom's specialized medical requirements, we were doing the right thing. Still, years later I had to process the guilt stuffed beneath my resentment—resentment toward my children for zapping my emotional and spiritual energy. All I can conclude is that work had become a temporary refuge, a place where I could lay aside the home front responsibilities for a few hours. So what if I traded one kind of stress for another?

In the end, of course, I unpacked the suitcase, and we worked things out. Still it wouldn't be the last time that, in the heat of bat-tle, we took potshots at each other. I wouldn't discover until years later that I wasn't the only one who had thought about leaving.

Sipping our coffee on the patio one morning, Jim scanned the newspaper while I sat thinking of last night's blowup, yet another with our eldest son, now an adult. Unbidden tears began coursing down my cheeks, tears that refused to stop. Once again my emo-tions were threatening to unleash. Jim never noticed and just kept leisurely leafing through the paper. *Surely he'll notice soon and at least reach out to take my hand,* I thought.

Page after page, he kept reading.

Finally I lashed out. "How can you just sit there when I'm in all this pain? Say something!"

He pitched the paper at a pot of geraniums. "What do you want me to say? We've been through this a hundred times, Judi. There's nothing more we can do."

"I'm not talking about the situation—I'm talking about *us*. This is tearing me apart, and you just sit there. You don't seem to be af-fected at all."

I stormed into the house, leaving him with his beloved paper.

A few minutes later he found me lying on the bed, staring red-eyed at the ceiling.

"Honey, let me tell you something. Just because I don't react the same way doesn't mean I don't feel the pain of this as deeply as you do."

I kept staring at the ceiling, unable to respond.

"Truth is, keeping busy is my way of dealing with it."

"That's part of the problem. You just seem to go on with life as if nothing were happening."

"I'm still here, aren't I?"

What was he getting at?

"If I had done what I really felt like," he said, keeping a level tone, "I would have been gone a long time ago. But I'm committed to sticking this out, Honey. To do that, I can't let feelings get the best of me. I have to deal with it in my own way."

In all our married years, I never had a clue that he felt that way, nor that he might not always be there. Suddenly I was grateful be-yond explanation.

Author Tom Mullen in his book *Seriously, Life Is a Laughing*

Matter writes, "Marriages are not made in heaven. They come in kits, and we put them together ourselves."[1] Adding to that, could it be that what you had in common early on isn't nearly as important as what you build together? And children, even or especially prodigal children, play an integral part—if you can hang in there through the stress.

When we got married we received a ton of wedding gifts. Moving into our first apartment, I felt an obligation to find a place for every one. For years we lugged them around from one parsonage to another. Of course, some got lost or broken along the way. Some we eventually pitched, realizing after a while that they simply created too much clutter.

Married life, we've discovered, is the same sorting-out process. We all come from different backgrounds, environments, and styles of upbringing, creating different personalities and viewpoints. Simply spoken, we all bring a lot of baggage with us into our relationships. Hopefully, the things that complement and balance are what we dust regularly and hold onto. Some things, however, it doesn't hurt to lose. And some we must make a deliberate effort to remove.

Then, of course, there are a few things we simply have to learn to live with. Interesting how what initially attracted us to each other can become an irritation, especially under stress. The first time I laid eyes on my husband, he had just returned to college from his second summer in Alaska serving as a missionary intern and working to make money for college. It was the late 1960s, and he was wearing a grubby green army jacket, floppy hat, and full beard. Thank goodness he cleaned up pretty well. What emerged was this handsome, independent, 20-year-old man of the world who had been places I had never even thought about. In the words of an old song, fascination soon turned to love.

How many times over the last 36 years that independent spirit turned my calm, controlled world upside down! And I won't even try to enumerate the ways my Scarlett O'Hara "I'll think about that tomorrow" temperament has frustrated my "Let's do it now, and let's do it this way," type-A husband. At the same time, living with him has caused me to stretch and grow into a more disciplined person. And I believe he would tell you that my phlegmatism also makes me quite "phlexible"—something that has served us well through many ministerial maneuvers. Anyway, wouldn't it be boring if we were all alike?

The problem is that it's a lifelong adjustment and learning process. And before we can master Marriage 101, the children usually come along. Even under normal circumstances, marriage and the years of raising a family can be overwhelming. Add to that the stress of developing a ministry. No wonder we don't always make the most informed decisions on either front. Later, when we're tempted to say to each other, "If you had only . . ." or "Maybe if I had known better than to . . ." or "Why didn't you see what was happening?" it may help to be reminded of a couple things. We made the best choices with the wisdom and information we had.

Or maybe we didn't.

Either way, sometimes the only thing to do is say, "OK, we made mistakes. Now how do we work together to fix it?" As Jim often says, "You can't drive forward while looking in the rearview mirror." There are times when a heartfelt apology gets us a lot farther down the road than a debate over who said what, when, and why.

As the prodigal years progressed, the fact that Jim and I are not just alike is probably what saved us. We each had our own way of dealing with things, which in most cases created balance. Just when one of us was ready to throw in the towel, the other would step into the ring. Interesting how one would have strength when the other was stressing. Only on rare occasions did we both hit rock bottom at the same time. I shudder to think about those times. In the long run, it took both our resources put together to survive.

Truth is, opposites can be great allies if they learn to accept and appreciate their differences and not undermine each other. It's OK to disagree in private as long as you present a united front. That's not always easy when it comes to a prodigal.

Yet another pastor's wife wrote about the problems that arose in their home when their son began dating a non-Christian girl. As things got more serious, his concerned parents counseled him to stop seeing her. When they pressed the issue, he became unruly, withdrawn, and angry. The day arrived when the pastor-husband felt he had no choice but to practice the tough love he had preached so often to others. He issued the ultimatum: give up the girlfriend, or get out. His wife went along, but tough love was hard on her tender heart.

"Boy, that was a hard decision to make, especially for me," she writes. "It was his senior year in high school, and he was just going to turn 18. We always had a special family gathering for the 18th birthday. I wanted to say it was OK for him to see her just so we could keep peace in the house. But I knew in my heart that we couldn't compromise."

No doubt about it. Those types of decisions are tough on a ministry and the marriage. Yet on good, bad, and indifferent days, we must honor the commitment we made to God and each other. One of the most difficult things my husband has to do as a denominational executive is look into the eyes of a minister who has lost his home, family, and ministry because of a marriage or moral failure. For our own sakes and that of our children and church, we must work to preserve our relationship at all costs.

And it doesn't all have to be work. Sometimes it helps just to take a reflective respite. Not only is it joyful, but it's also vital to a marriage that you take time every so often to remember where you started. What was it that brought you together? Who were you before having children? How did it happen when God called you together into ministry? Especially when the difficult years come, it's so easy to lose perspective and take things, not to mention each other, for granted. These reflections can serve to reassure us that we did not begin this journey on a whim and that nothing happened by accident. Oh, and just for the record—I still love that guy in the green army jacket.

Of course, husbands and wives are not the only ones God joins together.

Consider the story of our dear pastor friends John and Jacque DiGiacomo, who, unsuccessful in having biological children, chose to adopt Samuel. Only after he was ensconced in their home and hearts did they discover that, contrary to the initial report, his birth mother had done drugs during her pregnancy. As a result, Samuel suffered some emotional disorders that have led to social and behavioral problems, causing family heartache. But never once have I heard either John or Jacque express regret for the decision they made to keep Sam. Nor have they wavered in their commitment to loving him and giving spiritual guidance even after Jacque miraculously gave birth to their natural son, Dominick. To them this only served as confirmation of God's faithfulness and blessing for their decision to remain committed to their family and each other.

Another precious pastor writes about their difficult days with a son they received through a foreign adoption agency. From his earliest childhood, the boy displayed an incorrigible defiance. "It has been two years since we have seen Joe," he writes. Though he and his wife could easily choose to disown the boy who is now an adult, they remained hopeful, indicating they would still "gladly kill the fatted calf and receive him as a son."

Some children break your heart through no fault of their own. Pastor Chuck and Cheri Adams only recently lost their beautiful daughter, Courtney, age 19, to cancer. One has to wonder, *What if they had known? Would they still have chosen to have Courtney?*

"Yes," says Cherie, "without question. Though God only allowed Courtney to remain on earth for a short time, so many were touched by her life"—no one more than her older prodigal brother.

Chadwicke had begun to question his faith in college and for two years struggled to serve God. Learning of his sister's illness started him on the road back home. Only shortly before her death, he finally recommitted his life to the Lord. It was then that Courtney told her mother that she believed God used her illness to get Chadwicke's attention. Though deeply saddened by their loss, knowing that the family circle will be complete in heaven has given this inspiring ministry family joy and hope, something they continually give back to others.

Undoubtedly, having children means taking risks. Unlike toys or appliances, children don't come with guarantees. We look on the circumstances of our children's births, the different personalities, and the ensuing choices they make. Then, like Jesus' own mother, we ponder many things in our hearts. No matter—we love our children dearly. Why else would it be so painful?

"If raising children was supposed to be easy," quotes author Barbara Johnson, "it wouldn't have started with something called labor."[2] Our first son, the one who would be our biggest challenge, was ironically the only one we purposely planned. The year just prior, we had lost a baby through miscarriage, so when this pregnancy was successful, we were thrilled. We really, really wanted this child.

Number-two son was a bit of a surprise, conceived only 15

months later despite the use of contraceptives. However, any momentary misgivings melted when he was born with a congenital hip problem that required him to wear a burdensome leg brace for almost two years. This temporary disability only seemed to challenge him to try harder to keep up and prove himself, a trait we know will have benefits, especially as he channels his talent and energy in a divine direction.

If number-two son was a surprise, number-three child was a shock. Feeling two children were enough, we had taken surgical measures not to have more. Less than a year later, I was pregnant again, a fact I discovered while my husband was on a mission trip in the Philippines. I can still remember his words when I broke the news. "Well," he said with as much conviction as he could muster given the circumstances, "the Lord must want us to have three children." God has confirmed that many times over.

There are no two earthly relationships that reveal to us as much about God as that of husband and wife and parent and child: trust, intimacy, commitment, unconditional love, perseverance—just to name a few. Only by experiencing this particular brand of joy and pain can we truly comprehend the heart of our Heavenly Father, a father who continues to love and is willing to forgive no matter how many times He is rejected and hurt.

I can't begin to tell you what our children have taught us—and I mean that in the most positive sense—as God has been in the process over the years of weaving our family together. I have to admit that at times it's felt as if He were ripping out a few stitches. But that's because mistakes have to be corrected if you're going to end up with a top-quality garment.

Many times it has brought us to a place of naked humility where we have been forced to view ourselves honestly, our vulnerabilities and unrealistic expectations exposed. Though these may have produced some tough times of struggling with guilt and casting blame, by God's grace we survived and learned a lot about ourselves and each other along the way.

This has resulted in a deeper understanding of trusting God—especially when we don't feel like it. Knowing that God is still weaving the strands of our lives together, we joyfully anticipate a royal robe.

Lord, we thank You for each other, that in Your own providence

You chose to join our lives together. Let us never take for granted the miracle of our meeting or the family You've blessed us with. Never let us doubt Your divine plan or Your eternal purpose. Bind us together with cords of love that can never be broken. In Your name we pray. Amen.

Early in our marriage, prior to having children, Jim and I spent one year in a remote Alaskan fishing village pastoring a small mission. The village was located on an island accessible only by boat or plane and boasted about 90 full-time inhabitants, only six professing the Christian faith. I've always said that one year made our marriage and our ministry. When it came right down to it, we were pretty much all we had. There was little choice but to stay and work out our problems. So we learned what it meant to love, trust, and depend on each other. By the time we left, we knew one thing: if we could make it in that environment, we could probably make it anywhere.

Thirty-seven years later, it turns out we were right.

But that's not to say we didn't have a little help along the way.

The Weaver

My life is but a weaving
    Between my Lord and me.
I cannot choose the colors
    He worketh steadily.

Oftimes He weaveth sorrow,
    And I in foolish pride
Forget He sees the upper,
    And I, the underside.

Not until the loom is silent
    And the shuttles cease to fly
Shall God unroll the canvas
    And explain the reasons why.

The dark threads are as needful
    In the Weaver's skillful hand
As the threads of gold and silver
    In the pattern He has planned.
           —Author unknown

9

Hanging Between Heaven and Help

A wise man will hear, and will increase learning; and a man of understanding shall attain unto wise counsels.
—Prov. 1:5, KJV

Some family vacations become memorable for all the wrong reasons. When our boys were ages eight, six, and three, we joined another family for a motor-home trip through Canada, our eventual destination being Anchorage, Alaska. Two days into the trip, we were deep in the scenic but secluded Canadian wilderness. It was late the second afternoon when, having seen little but woods and wildlife, we finally came on a good-sized campground and rest area complete with kids' playground. Not 30 minutes later, our youngest son fell off the monkey bars and broke his arm.

The proprietor loaded us up with Tylenol with codeine and pointed us to the nearest clinic—two hours back down the winding road that we had just driven. Praying all the way, we headed for the hospital, wondering what we would find when we got there. It was two tortuous, twisting hours of hanging between heaven and help.

Thankfully, we found a clean, well-equipped clinic with a competent, compassionate doctor—a pleasant fellow with a German accent who appeared in the middle of the night wearing Bermuda shorts and clogs. Faster than our wild mountain ride, our son's arm was set in a cast and we were back on the road. And the total bill? It came to only $150 U.S. dollars—a serendipitous surprise. Still, I can tell you with certainty that we would have gladly paid whatever it cost.

Now let me ask you this. What would you think of our parenting skills if, despite our son's distress, we had decided to hop back in the motor home and keep driving toward Anchorage? *Terrible.*

Ridiculous. Irresponsible. You're right. Any parent would do exactly what we did—get assistance quickly and pay whatever it cost to patch up their kid.

Why, then, when we see our families in emotional distress, are many ministers so often reluctant to seek immediate professional counseling?

Initially perhaps, it's that "D" word again: *denial.* Either we don't recognize that we have a problem, or we may not consider the situation bad enough to merit professional help. Oh, sure, we've hit a little bump in the road, but that goes with the terrain, right? Yes, until you discover there's more to the bump than meets the eye.

Due to the weather extremes—freezing and thawing—Alaskan roads are notorious for potholes. Once, during a spring rain, I drove over what appeared to be a large puddle in the road. Instead, I sunk into a huge pothole filled with water. *Thunk. Crunch. Sssst.* Not only was my tire flat, but the metal rim was buckled as well. How I cringed thinking of calling Jim to explain. But there was no denying it—the car wouldn't budge without professional help.

Likewise, only when we plop into a major personal pothole and are dragged out, dents and all, do we begin to consider the need for outside intervention.

Enter then the "P" word: *pride.* What will people—our congregation or other ministers in particular—think if they find out we're going to a counselor? *What? The preacher needs a shrink?* After all, we're the ones who counsel others. If we're supplying them with answers, why can't we dole a few out to ourselves?

For one thing, it's impossible for us to be objective and impartial. Not when we're so personally involved, and—perish the thought—maybe even part of the problem. (And what if a hint of that leaks out?) Another truth is that our children are more prone to open their ears to advice when it comes from someone else, something my husband found out the hard way.

One day Jim sat down to hash out some thorny issue with our middle son. For about ten minutes he employed his best counseling and communication skills. Finally, feeling he had done a more-than-adequate job of dissecting the dilemma, he paused to give the boy a chance to respond.

"So, Dad," our unimpressed son said flatly, "what's your point?"

That's when Jim felt like the elderly parson arriving at the second point of his sermon only to find it made no point at all.

Long before that incident, my husband had concluded that his counseling should be limited to his area of expertise, the Bible. Thus he eventually made it his policy to schedule a maximum of three meetings with counsel-seekers to listen, explain scriptural principles, offer spiritual guidance or moral advice, and pray. In that sense we can counsel ourselves to some extent. We know the scripture and should be able to apply it to our own lives. We can and do pray. Issues requiring psychological or long-term counseling, however, Jim referred to the well trained and capable who specialize in it. It's a wise pastor who recognizes his limitations—both in time and talent—and is willing to refer someone so he or she can receive the help that's really needed.

So why are we reluctant to refer ourselves?

Certainly it requires some hard-fought humility to say to someone, "I can't fix this myself. Can you help me?" For many of us minister-types, the rim must be badly bent before we'll lay aside our pride and send out the SOS.

That's why, to preserve our dignity, we would often rather just go the self-help route.

If there's one thing we ministry folks are famous for, it's attending conferences and seminars. There's much to be gleaned from a good marriage-and-family conference. It's just that sometimes it's overwhelming to ferret out what pertains to our situation and apply it correctly. Let's be honest—we're prone to frequent these seminars not so much to explore what's wrong with ourselves but to pinpoint the problems of the other person. Some of us even pack along the wrong attitude that it applies to everyone *but* us. Our best hope is to come away inspired and convicted to take some personal action toward improvement. But without some follow-up, it's usually a temporary fix. By nature, most conferences and seminars are limited in their ability to personalize to the point of meeting specific needs.

So we turn to books dealing with marriage and family, written by authors like me who hope to inspire and encourage from their own mutual fund of experience. Over the years, I've read many cover to cover, finding much encouragement. If I'm honest, though, I must admit that the most enjoyable ones offered more hope than help. They contained inspiring stories, testimonials, and poignant devotionals. Least helpful, at least for me, were those preventative or formulaic in nature.

Take two scriptures a day, hug your child three times, go to a Tough Love meeting, and put a lock on his or her door.

Maybe it was because at that point in our journey it was too late for counteractive measures and suggested blanket remedies. In our desperation we were undoubtedly looking for guarantees of success. If the formulas didn't pan out, it would only lead to more disappointment. *Why isn't this working for us? Didn't we apply the prescription correctly?* Again, this is only my personal experience.

Another way we find help and comfort is to talk and pray with other pastors and individuals going through similar deep waters. What a relief and encouragement just to know that we in ministry aren't alone in facing this particular problem! For years, Jim and I felt as if we were working underground to rescue our family. In many ways it helped to come out of the closet and compare notes with others in this form of *secret service.*

What doesn't help is when these informal forums become a free-for-all in which we hash over the same old pain with no suggested battle plan, or worse yet, a place for sharing collective misinformation. While we're all good at joint commiserating, we aren't always able to offer sure-fix solutions. This is a point worth remembering as prodigal prayer and support groups now seem to be popping up everywhere, not to mention the ever-expanding Internet, which offers unlimited chat connection to others with like needs.

Then there's the privacy issue. For those in ministry to whom confidentiality is still an understandable concern, any open forum is potentially problematic.

Beware, too, the new gurus of pop psychology. While many of us may find Dr. Phil or some like-minded media medic entertaining, it's wise to remember that's what most of them are being paid to do—entertain. Trying to apply that type of one-size-fits-all therapy is like taking someone else's pills.

While these may all be useful tools in helping us cope, the one recurring theme in every form of self-help is that none can be easily personalized. You have to wade through a lot of information to find the bits that apply to your specific situation. That's why there's nothing that takes the place of sitting down with a person professionally trained to know what to look and listen for, a person who can help you understand yourself and your situation better. A good Christian counselor will not only point out what you may have done wrong but also affirm what you're doing right, then prayerfully offer skills to apply like ointment to the wound.

Still, the same way some people resist seeing the doctor in case it's bad news, some of us will resist seeking professional counseling. Is it because we're afraid to find out what's wrong, or that we view it as admitting to failure? Either way, the longer we wait, the more intensive and expensive the treatment.

Mel Johnson is a minister and California state-licensed marriage and family therapist who, along with his wife, Sharon, established Rekindle Ministries, a counseling service they offer free of charge to ministers and missionaries. Supported by their own retirement income and donations, these wonderful folks have been a blessing to hundreds of ministry families at home and abroad over the last several years.

Listen to what Mel says: "One of the greatest problems I face as a counselor is the delay that turns a solvable problem into a basket case. 'If only we had sought help sooner' is a statement I've heard hundreds of times. It's true that what can be solved with a band-aid today will probably require major surgery tomorrow."

My minister friend Robin Williams-Aladeen runs a busy and successful counseling service in the heart of San Francisco. Robin has built her clientele list to include many ministers. "Every day I deal with situations that could have been avoided if they had sought counseling earlier," she echoes. "Pastors and their families would be well served to find a good family therapist before they need one, one that's a good fit for your family."

Her urging is that every ministry family would "go in for a checkup," kind of like getting a good doctor or dentist on board before the crisis. "It's an hour or two well spent."

Why? "Because," Robin explains, "it sends a message to the spouse and kids that counseling is not just a last resort but a healthy, helpful, and nonthreatening way to make sure you're communicating. It also allows the family to deal with any stuff from family of origin that Mom or Dad brought to the marriage."

Now there's a thought to chew on.

Our family was a prime example. By the time it became apparent that we had a problem meriting outside help, everything was directed at our son. He was the source of the problem, right? He needs to be fixed. If only we could find the right counselor to make him see the error of his ways, to point out how he was hurting himself and us. We were in pain and looking for a quick fix. No wonder when one counselor began delving into Jim's and my upbringing we couldn't understand why the guy was wasting precious time (and money). Let's find someone with a "more direct approach," we agreed—a search that found us dragging our poor son through a plethora of professionals. *This one's a bit too mellow. That one's too confrontational.* How much sooner might we all have benefited if we had had a known and trusted counselor already on board—and had seen the need to pursue some previous, proactive counsel!

Truth was, like many couples, Jim and I were still working out some personal differences. Both of us were last-born children and were each admittedly a bit spoiled and selfish—not to mention immature. I was only 18 when we married and had never lived on my own except for one year in the college dorm. I can see now how I transferred a lot of dependence onto my "much older and wiser" 21-year-old husband. He probably wondered many times in those early years what he had gotten himself into but gallantly rose to the task. As our marriage progressed, I naturally began asserting myself more. No surprise that by the time the kids came along, there was some confusion in the area of control, along with a number of other unresolved issues.

This included poor communication skills. Because Jim and I had very different ways of processing, it was hard for us to discuss things without becoming defensive. Consequently, we took on the habit of waiting until crisis forced us into confrontation. Then inevitably other latent issues would surface. No wonder under the pressure of a prodigal we ended up with more problems than we bargained for both as a couple and as a family.

Aren't you sorry to learn that our family was so dysfunctional? Before feeling too bad, you might want to take a good honest look around. Truth is, every family, ministry families included, is dysfunctional to some extent. Why? Because every family is human. How we all need God's grace and forgiveness every single day!

This brings us to the real root of the struggle many have with seeking professional counsel. Too often it's a sad carryover from the long prevailing assumption that "good" Christians don't have that magnitude of problems. Could our real concern with seeking psychological counsel be that it may indicate either personal failure or lack of faith and thus be construed to our congregations and others as (gasp!) unspiritual?

Let me share again some excellent words of insight from our friend Mel Johnson. "It's called honesty when we acknowledge our problems," he says. "That's to a person's credit, not discredit. The best role model we can set for our congregations is to be honest. What can possibly be more spiritual than that?"

Simply put, if we're dishonest, we deceive not only ourselves but others. At the same time we keep our families from receiving the help they need.

And what about its being a lack of faith? Here again is Mel's practical and proven observation: "Christians, even ministers, sometimes have a limited concept of how God works, or can work, to help His children. They insist that God must take care of their problem in a prescribed way, i.e., miraculously or in some other stereotypical, often inexplicable way. 'We're trusting God,' we say. 'God will take care of it in His own way and time.' So we just wait, feeling that doing anything else would show a lack of faith."

Fortunately this attitude has changed a lot over the years. After all, we believe in divine healing, but most of us still seek the services of a doctor. What makes this any different?

"The bottom line is this," Mel continues. "God is sovereign. He is at liberty to meet people's needs in whatever way He chooses. It may help to be reminded that God has historically chosen to help us through another. He won't hold it against us if we seek help.

"And let's be honest, God sometimes seems far removed and untouchable. We need human contact. Laying hands on the sick is scriptural. It can be a comforting thing when you feel that your 'illness' has isolated you from others. There's simply no reason any of us should go through this alone."

"Counseling," Mel concludes, "is in some cases the most spiritual thing that can be done."

So does that mean we stop trusting God and place our total trust in human beings? No. It simply means trusting God to direct us to the person who is best trained to help us, asking Him all along the way for the humility to admit our shortcomings and wisdom to apply the tools that therapy offers to help remedy our situation.

To that I'll add a couple of personal observations. It's common in the space of waiting for God to answer the prayers for our prodigal that we feel helpless, or that in seeking to do the right thing—or anything—we end up losing control and saying or doing something that exacerbates the situation, resulting in even more feelings of failure and helplessness. A counselor can give us verbal and emotional tools that help us handle the day-to-day dilemmas and feel more in control (the good kind). Also, it's been my experience that it's better to seek the counsel of a trained professional than too many well-meaning others who may even give conflicting counsel, only leading to more hurt and confusion.

So how do we know when to seek counseling? Mel offers the following guidelines. When

- we've repeatedly tried to solve the problem but without success.
- attempts to solve the problem have encountered resistance from other involved parties.
- the home atmosphere is so emotionally charged over the problem that no progress can be made.
- we have come to a clear understanding that we don't have the resources, motivation, understanding, and so on to adequately cope with the problem.

We've navigated past a few of the daunting detours we may find on the road between heaven and help. Now, however, we come to what is undoubtedly a major roadblock for many of us. There's no getting around this one without being honest; ongoing counseling can be expensive. *How can we afford it,* we wonder, *living on a minister's meager income?*

So exactly how much are we talking here?

According to Robin Williams-Aladeen, therapy costs can run the gamut between pro bono (free), adjusted clergy rates, to a full fee of as much as $250 a session. "The general fee is going to be somewhere between $75 and $125 an hour if you see a psychologist," she states. "If you choose to see a psychiatrist, the fees might run closer to $200."

Before you choke, read on.

What's the standard difference between the two? A psychiatrist has a medical doctor's degree and can prescribe medication if the situation warrants it.

But take heart. Robin's counsel is that most clergy would be served well to see either a psychologist or marriage, family, and child counselor, which means you're looking at the lower end of the fee scale.

Some additional advice she offers is to always ask if a counselor sees pastors and/or their families at a special rate, as many Christian therapists do. "In the initial phone consultation when you're setting the appointment, you're within rights to tell the counselor what you're prepared to pay and ask whether the therapist can work with that. If not, it's appropriate to ask for the name of a therapist who may be able to meet your financial constraints. Keep in mind, however, that some Christian therapists are able to carry only a limited number of reduced-rate cases at one time."

Still struggling to see how you can stretch the already see-through budget?

Consider another practical observation from Mel Johnson: "The money issue is usually a rationalization. Most people have money to spend where they want to spend it. It's a matter of priorities. When our car needs new tires, we put out the dollars because it's a high priority. Too often relationships, family stability, and emotional growth don't rank up there with new tires."

It may require some sacrifice, but again, allow me to note something from my personal perspective: counselor fees were nothing compared to the $10,000 we paid for our son's unsuccessful stint in drug rehabilitation.

Now we come to the question that presents the most legitimate lag when it comes to pursuing family counseling: "Whom do we call?" The important things to a ministry family are to find someone with objectivity, confidentiality, and no conflict of interests. Never use anyone who is not a Christian, and be sure to pick someone who agrees closely with your doctrinal views.

Both Mel and Robin agree that the best place to start is to call another pastor in the area or ask friends. You can also check the phonebook for Christian counseling centers. Or go on the Internet to the American Association of Christian Counselors (aacc.net) and do a search by ZIP code or city.

Citing the legitimate concern many pastors have regarding a possible breech of confidentiality, Robin encourages that it may give pastors and their families peace of mind to seek a therapist outside their own denominational family. "A Nazarene pastor may be well served to call the local Baptist or Presbyterian church to ask for a referral, the Baptist pastor may want to call the local Congregational church, and so on." The thing she stresses is to choose someone who has a sympathetic understanding of the unique pressures the pastor's family encounters.

Increasingly there are people with credentialed ministry backgrounds who are ministering full time as professionally trained therapists. They provide extremely practical insights because they truly do understand firsthand pastoral pressures and the special heartache of sons and daughters who are breaking away from the home and spiritual structure. Both Mel and Robin stress the importance of finding the right fit.

"After locating a possible counselor," Mel advises, "make sure you speak directly with him or her by phone, sharing concerns about counseling and asking any questions you may have, especially those regarding doctrine, counseling theory or approach, training and experience, and fees."

Robin takes it a step further. "Be prepared to meet initially with several counselors. Ideally, you may want to set up 15-minute appointments with three different therapists (both male and female) and meet them personally. If you have a strong preference for one of the three, then ask your spouse to join you and have a full hour together with the therapist to see if you both feel this is a good match for your family and the issues you're facing."

She suggests some questions that should be settled in that initial interview:

- Did you have a good feeling about the therapist? Do you like him or her? Is this individual easy to talk with? Do you feel comfortable asking the therapist to pray with you over the situation? Did he or she seem to ask enough questions, or did you feel he or she talked down to you about what you should do?
- How many other ministry families has this therapist seen?
- Is the office in a location that preserves your confidentiality, i.e. a professional building versus a church office? Did you

feel comfortable meeting in the office? Was the office clean and inviting?

Remember—you're the customer. You're paying a fee, and you want the optimum for your money. You deserve a place where you feel safe, professional, and open.

Here's another consideration when it comes to getting the most for your money. One time I made a counseling appointment for our family, only to discover at the last minute that our son was unwilling to go. My initial inclination was to cancel the whole thing. After all, it's going to work only if all parties involved are present and willing to participate, right? That's the ideal. So why waste the money?

Still I felt let down. That's when I decided, *No, I'll go it alone.* It turned out to be worth every penny. I ended up giving myself a personal gift of affirmation, positive support, and much-needed individualized coping skills. Thanks to the expertise, objectivity, and loving concern of a wonderful Christian counselor, I came away from the session with a clearer perspective on our circumstances and feeling better equipped to deal with whatever was waiting at home.

My meeting with the Christian counselor ultimately profited the whole family.

Counseling gives us a safe open forum for sorting thoughts and feelings honestly. Even more, it allows us to see our circumstances through the eyes of someone who's trained to pinpoint problems. This sometimes enables us to see God's divine direction more clearly. In this way our minds are freed to arrive at our own Spirit-inspired solutions for dealing with difficult situations. This perhaps accounts for an episode that proved to be a turning point in my ongoing effort to find a better avenue of communication with our oldest son.

Many of the clashes between the two of us stemmed not from being different but from being too much alike in ways. Because both of us are emotional and at times quick to react, it didn't take long for us to learn how to push each other's buttons. This resulted in a lot of highly charged but completely unproductive discussions.

It was following one of these, after our son had once again stormed out of the house in angry frustration, that the Lord gave me an inspiration. After a good hearty cry, I decided to write my son a letter and leave it on his pillow. Sure enough, a few days later I received a written reply. In the lines of that note were glimpses of the son I thought was lost.

Mom, I've caused you to resent me for a lot of things, and I'm sorry. . . . I hope we can get some things worked out. . . . I appreciate your love and care. . . . I love you (and Dad) both.

Many times after that when we reached a verbal impasse, we wrote notes to each other. It allowed time to choose exactly what we wanted to say, making changes if necessary; then the other person could compose a thoughtful, not just reactive, response. I kept a number of these notes, along with other cards we received from all our sons over the years. Even now, coming across them encourages me to remember that a lot more is going on than we sometimes see.

Lord, we fully acknowledge that You are the Great Counselor. Help us first and foremost to depend on Your divine direction and wisdom. We thank You for those in the Body of Christ who have applied themselves to learning and committed themselves to compassion. Give us humility to admit that sometimes we simply need someone else, then courage to ask for help when we need it, and finally, wisdom to assess and apply the counsel we're given. In Jesus' name. Amen.

It's never too late to seek out a good Christian counselor. Jim and I had been married 34 years—long after our boys had all left home—when we hit a small snag resulting from some midlife transitions. This time, it had nothing to do with our children, though I'm sure there were some leftover lesions from those difficult years. It was more a sense that we were entering a new season of life and didn't want to drag the old repetitive rubs with us. "Despite the difficult times," I told the counselor, "we've had a good marriage and a great life together. The reason we're here now is to make sure we finish even stronger than we started."

Besides that, I think both of us needed to know what remained of that optimistic young couple who long ago walked hand-in-hand across that Bible school campus.

Our counselor recommended that we take the Meyers-Briggs Temperament Analysis test. Since we had never done anything like that before, I was a bit apprehensive. *What is this supposed to prove? What if it doesn't pan out? Thirty-four years is a little late for an annulment.* Not surprisingly, our scores revealed a number of personality differences. However, the counselor helped us see how our different ways of seeing and doing things had brought balance in many important ways over the years. That was reassuring. We were also assured that it's OK to view things differently; it doesn't mean either of us is always right or wrong.

Now why didn't someone tell us that 34 years ago? Perhaps because we never asked.

"The important thing," the counselor emphasized, "is that you love God, are committed to each other, and continue using your individual gifts to achieve the same goal." That, of course, is what has kept us going all these years. "At the same time," she went on, "it's important to support each other's individual interests." OK. We can do that.

You know how you feel when you finally get around to asking the doctor about some niggling, nagging ache or pain—the kind you worry about but keep dismissing as gas or arthritis? That's how I felt coming out of the counselor's office that day. Whether the diagnosis is "It's nothing to worry about" or "Maybe we should just run a couple of tests," at least you know where to go from there.

And doesn't it still boil down to hanging onto heaven? Even if it means you sometimes need a little help.

10

The Long Road Home

An early 1990s entry in my journal reads as follows:

Last night I dreamed I was at Universal Studios standing in line for the "Jaws" attraction. This is the one where you get in a boat knowing that somewhere along the way you'll encounter the gigantic white shark of movie fame. I remember thinking as I shuffled along, *What am I doing? I hate these scary rides.* But when the boat came, I was caught in the crowd and forced on.

For the first part of the ride I cowered in the middle, hoping by doing so I wouldn't have to come face-to-face with the monster. At one point I caught a frightening, far-away glimpse of the big fish. Then before anything else could happen, the boat came to a docking station. Here the guide announced that everyone should get off and decide whether he or she wanted to catch the next boat and finish the ride. Oh, how I wanted to exit and find the merry-go-round!

But something inside said, *No, you're going to finish this ride. It's only scary because you don't know what's going to happen.* Somehow I knew that although the ride is designed to bring you face-to-face with "Jaws," he wouldn't be allowed to capsize the boat. After all, if that happened the ride would be over.

Just then another boat pulled up to the dock, I stepped on, and . . .

That's when I woke up.

I have to tell you that I am not the kind of person who puts a lot of stock in dreams. Only once or twice have I ever felt God used a dream to speak to me; each time it was a confirmation of something I already knew to be true. But I don't deny their sometimes symbolic significance either. After all, weren't there a number of times in the Bible when God used dreams to reveal important or prophetic truths? It's certain that dreams often serve to surface what's going on in our subconscious. Either way, whether it was God or Memorex, my virtual vision struck me as significant enough to record it in my journal.

Up until the time we left Sacramento I had been convinced that it couldn't be much longer before our oldest son "came to his senses" and got his life straightened out. I was sure when the transformation happened he would make a sudden 180-degree turn, come home, and our life as a family would take up where it had left off three years before.

By the time we had been in our new church position for a year, it was becoming apparent that the "ride" with both older boys was a long way from over. Our oldest son was still living with his girlfriend and involved in the skinhead scene and partying hard. If there was one small positive, it was that he now faced the reality that he had to work to support himself.

Our middle son's tenure with the church family that took him in lasted only a few weeks. He soon discovered that the rules there were even more restrictive than home. He paid us one short visit to check things out, but it didn't take long to decide that our new situation wasn't for him. At loose ends, he returned to Sacramento, dropped out of school, and got a fast-food job and an apartment that basically served as a hangout and party place.

For us the good thing about being so far away was that we couldn't see what was going on, so we were no longer as tempted to intervene. Sometimes we could even get through a string of days without worrying and wondering. Then a crisis phone call would come from one of the boys to jangle us out of bed and back into reality. Now, however, we couldn't just drop everything and run. Instead we'd do our best to counsel, then hang up and pray that God would continue to use the consequences of their choices to reach them. It wasn't easy.

Periodic visits to Sacramento confirmed that the conditions hadn't improved much. Each time we would return home with new concerns and heavy hearts. No wonder my worst fears, which had been circling like a great white shark, finally surfaced in the night.

Ironically, however, as the dream brought me face-to-face with some monster misgivings, a number of things became clear. Obviously I felt that, at some point, I had been forced onto a ride I didn't want to be on. And it was frightening. My natural reaction had been to cower in the boat hoping that our disconcerting circumstances were short-lived and that the ride would soon be over.

Then came the docking place—a point of significant shift.

Now it seemed I was being given a choice: not whether, but how I would finish the ride! Truth is, I couldn't have gotten off if I wanted to. Willing or not, I still had to find a way out of that dark place. Here's where I believe the Lord used the dream to show me three things:

- No matter what happened on the ride, He would be with me in the boat.
- We would make it to the end without being capsized.
- It was up to me as to whether to ride it out in fear or to ride it out in faith.

That's when it hit me that this could be an elongated expedition.

Though we hadn't fully realized it, we had come to a place of transition in life as well. Obviously the separation from our two older sons was not what we would have chosen. But the Lord knew we couldn't go on living the way things were. It was time for us to see our children separate from ourselves and understand that God was still working in all our lives, just in different ways.

I believe He also knew the only way we could be removed emotionally was to be moved physically. We needed to see ourselves apart from the pain, to see that God still wanted to prosper us regardless of what our children were doing. In order to accomplish that, we needed a place that didn't know our children's history.

So we settled into our new home and church. Again, God blessed us with a congregation that embraced my husband's style of ministry and a staff that fit like a glove. I became involved once more in Sunday School teaching, music, and women's ministries. The active and energetic youth group provided a nurturing atmosphere for our youngest son, something I'll always credit as a contribution to the positive direction his life eventually took. Though we ended up staying there only two years, I know God provided this time as a healing transition. It was a time when we could step back far enough from the forest to once again see the individual beauty of the trees.

No doubt, a God's-eye glimpse can keep us going, as pastor's wife Sharon Strickland learned.

"There were days so difficult that I could only see what was facing me at the current time," she states, describing the circumstances surrounding their own prodigal. "I had to remind myself every day that God sees the big picture and that if we are faithful to Him and His word, He will be faithful to us."

In our case, I like to imagine God having more of an IMAX experience—as we would soon discover.

Even as Jim threw himself into casting a vision and direction for our new church—which had been without a pastor for a year prior to our coming—God was working behind the scenes in ways we could never imagine. It wasn't long into our tenure when the first hint arrived.

I was in the bedroom of our new house unpacking boxes the day Jim came home waving the letter. Actually it was our new *old* house, a remodeled and refurbished 106-year-old Victorian, something I had always dreamed of owning.

"You'll never believe what came in the mail today." The excitement in his voice carried all the way from the front parlor. Before I could ask, he went on. "It's a letter from the district office."

The head honchos? Must be special for him to be this jazzed. "What is it? Do they want you on some committee or the other?"

"Even better," he chortled. "What would you say if I tell you they're considering me for the position of district Christian education director?"

I looked around at the floral wallpaper, hand-carved doorframes, and laced-covered, leaded glass windows. "I don't want to talk about it."

But, of course, we did—and agreed it was an opportunity he shouldn't pass up.

Due to some district-level restructuring, it was two years before Jim assumed his new post, two years that God graciously allowed me to enjoy decorating and living in the beloved old Victorian. In the meantime, Jim worked fervently to stabilize the church, introduce new ministries, and prepare them for the transition. Though more short-lived than anticipated, it was a blessed and happy hiatus.

During this time God also brought to pass another of my own latent longings. I had my first writing piece published, giving me the inspiration and courage to shoulder again a serious pursuit of writing—something I had laid aside as the previous three years of turmoil drained my reservoir of creative energy.

Isn't it amazing how God delights in choosing just the right time to deliver even the smallest desires of our hearts? He was truly restoring our souls—and preparing us for the next interesting chain of events.

By the summer of 1993 my husband was ensconced in his new position and thoroughly enjoying his responsibilities to the 435 churches in our district. We had moved again, this time to a beautiful little town in the Santa Cruz Mountains where our district college and corporate offices were located. Surrounded by towering redwoods and pines, it was only a 15-minute sloping drive to the Pacific Ocean, an aesthetically peaceful place to live. The back porch of our two-bedroom bungalow led onto a long yard bordered by open pasture and overlooked the entire valley. God had definitely made a fair trade for the Victorian.

I took an open secretarial position in the district office. Our youngest son was finishing high school and was very involved in a local church. Though the older boys' living conditions were about the same, by now the crisis calls were fewer and farther between. In that setting, it was easy to believe that things were settling down.

That was—until we received the call from our oldest son informing us his girlfriend was pregnant and they had decided to get married.

The September wedding was held at our former church in Sacramento and was a fairly happy affair under the circumstances. It gave us a chance to see many of our beloved congregation who, ever supportive, came out in full force for the festivities.

Only afterward did reality sink in. In the spring we were going to be grandparents. And we were in-laws—the pending birth of our grandchild now bound us irrevocably to the young woman whom our son had left drug rehab to live with.

Lord, would the adjustments never end? Not any time soon.

It was only a few months later when our middle son announced that he and his new girlfriend, whom we hardly knew, were also expecting. As if one set of challenges weren't enough; now they were multiplying like rabbits.

On top of that, what would have previously played out on a local church platform took to the Broadway stage with Jim's very visual district position. Now instead of wondering what one congregation would think, we had 435 churches to consider. But God with his IMAX oversight had placed us in this position knowing full well our situation, right? Still it's not an easy thing to feel the whole world watching what you hoped would be a private performance. Even an inveterate virtuoso can become stage shy under those conditions.

My friend Christy Carr (not her real name) is a talented and dedicated pastor's wife with a definite dramatic and comedic flair, something God has used to produce her much-in-demand ministry revolving around speaking, singing, and pulpit-prone puppetry. You can imagine her pain and struggle upon learning of her 16-year-old daughter's unplanned pregnancy.

"At first I asked the Lord why," says Christy. "Then, couldn't He please do 'something' about the pregnancy? Women lose babies every day. Couldn't He do that for us, too? Then our lives could return to normal and our daughter could continue her childhood."

But God quickly shined His scriptural spotlight on her all-too-real-life drama.

"God showed me very clearly that though the sin was not His plan, He was the creator of life. Suddenly, all I knew from His Word came flooding into my mind. *We are fearfully and wonderfully made. He knows us before we are born. He's already planned our days.* I still didn't understand why this happened but began to trust that God would walk through it with me."

And He did. Following God's leading, Christy took a year away from her ministry to walk through that difficult time with her daughter. But that was only Act One. In the ensuing years Christy's life script would include her daughter's marriage and eventual divorce, a personal bout with cancer, the birth of another grandchild, and most recently, a painful parting from the church she and her husband had pastored for more than 20 years.

Yet through it all God has continued to bless and expand their ministry. Why? Because of the godly way they've chosen to allow the events of their lives to play out, providing for their daughter's physical and spiritual needs, loving and speaking into the lives of their grandchildren, then employing some tough love principles as the situation required—and showing incredible grace during their congregational conflict, even in the midst of their own distress. I can tell you after recently hearing Christy speak that she's an amazing inspiration as she openly shares with others what God has revealed in and through her life. And I can assure you, it's no act.

The longer our children wander, the more complicated things become. The more complicated things become, the more we must ask God for special wisdom to know how much to intervene. We want so much to keep giving our children chances to straighten up and fly right. The problem is that we're not always objective enough to determine whether they've really come to their senses or are just looking for means to continue living in the foreign land. The latter, we know, most often ends up involving a pigpen.

So we steel ourselves, trying hard to back off and allow them to make their own choices and then suffer the consequences. We pray and hope that at some point they'll get tired and hungry enough to begin taking responsibility for their own actions. The place where the lines sometimes blur is between allowing and assisting them in those choices, something that becomes even more difficult to determine as grandchildren arrive to fill in the family photo.

We've always made it clear to our children that we're willing to help them when they ask for it. The question requiring Solomon's wisdom is when to intercede and how best to help. There's never been a question that we would gladly provide for their basic physical needs—food, clothing, medical treatment. We've also tried to be generous in our emotional support—encouragement, forgiveness, practical and spiritual advice. But when it comes to the issue of giving them money, we learned the hard way to be cautious. When we've helped financially, we've done so prayerfully and practically, trying not to give the money directly in most cases.

Sadly, heart-wrenchingly, we have to let them live in the foreign land long enough not to want to be there anymore, all the while praying that God spares them, physically and spiritually. Again, this becomes especially hard when their lifestyles begin to affect their own children.

That makes staying connected not only important but integral.

We've kept out hearts and home open, making it clear that anyone at any time is welcome as long as he or she understands that it's a privilege requiring respect for rules and other family members. Even in the far corners of the distant land, they know we'll always regard them as a permanent part of the family unit. And we've discovered an amazing thing—there's no limit to how far heartstrings will stretch. Nor do they lose their strength to draw a prodigal home.

So it was, all those years ago as Jim and I found ourselves once again faced with new and critical choices involving our children and future grandchildren, that we made a double determination. High visibility or not, we would do what seemed best for our family and let God take care of the rest. It felt as if we were back at the docking place from my dream deciding again how to ride out this jog of the journey. Only this time there was no hesitation. Hand in hand, we jumped back into the boat, praying that we were prepared for whatever the remaining ride revealed.

For us that meant treating whomever God brought into our family, through whatever circumstances, as one of our own. Ten years, two daughters-in-law, four grandchildren, one divorce, and many interesting asides later, I believe we've done our best to do that. No doubt it has made at times for a tumultuous thrill ride. But let me also tell you how it has paid off.

First, if you open your heart, you find there's a lot more to people than what's visible on the skin. Once the grandchildren came along, both of our daughters-in-law cleaned up their lives and proved to be excellent mothers. After we got to know them, we discovered they were bright and creative, with sensitive hearts and many good qualities. A few times we've joked about keeping them and getting rid of our sons.

I've often said that God gave me an Orpah and a Ruth. Both girls came from divorced homes and unchurched backgrounds, so there have been many opportunities over the years to speak words of encouragement and healing into their lives. Unfortunately, we're separated from our first daughter-in-law now through divorce, though our grandchildren keep us in contact. The second has hung in there with us. Today not only are we great friends, but she's also proven to be a special help and blessing in so many ways.

Here is the greatest reward. Regardless of what's transpired in our children's lives, we've been able to stay closely connected with our four precious grandchildren. God has created a special bond between us and allowed us to consistently interject a Christian influence in their lives. And what joy they have given us! As events have unfolded, I can tell you without hesitation that, though life doesn't always turn out the way we planned, God's hand is always in it. And we can be part of it if we'll stay in the boat.

Today our three boys have gone very different directions. In 1994 our oldest son and his wife had a second child. It finally became apparent that if they were to stay together, some changes were needed. This necessitated a break from the old crowd, so they decided to move to Idaho, where she had relatives. It was a good decision in many ways and seemed for a while that they were making some positive progress. However, a few years and more bad decisions later, the marriage ended in divorce. For the sake of his children, our son decided to stay there and is working at putting his life back together. He's still living with the consequences of some continued errors in judgment, as we all are.

Now 33 years old, he laments the loss of his teenage years and the need for skills he should have developed then. He's hoping to develop those skills through vocational training. We're praying that as he continues to make better choices, it will help his shattered self-esteem. But most important, we hope that he'll soon choose to surrender his life back to the Lord.

After their baby was born, our middle son and his girlfriend got married. They have weathered a few stormy years but are still together. Now they have two precious children and live close by. He did eventually go back and finish high school, then made a few false starts toward getting a college degree. He has currently put that aside in order to pursue a promising career opportunity as a manager with Starbuck's. We continue to believe and pray that he, ever the analytical one, is seriously weighing some positive spiritual options.

Our youngest son went through a short rebellion during the years when we lived in the Santa Cruz area. I would call it more of a questioning time and coming of age. Through it all, however, he remained involved in church and attended a number of Christian youth camps. You can imagine our happiness when he came home from one such camp, asked our forgiveness for his rebellion, and informed us that he was planning to attend Bible college. We attended his graduation last spring, and he's now a full-time youth pastor in a church near San Francisco.

God has enabled us to love our children through many struggles. We believe God is at work in their lives and has a great plan for them individually and our family as a whole.

How has all this affected our personal ministry? Jim spent five years as our denomination's district Christian education director before being elected to the office of assistant superintendent, then advancing to superintendent. In April 2005 he will celebrate 12 years as a district official, following 25 years of pastoral ministry. All this is to say that God has opened doors we never imagined, allowing us to share His good news and encouragement around the world.

As for me, the Lord has graciously expanded my own ministry in the area of speaking and writing. Last year, with my husband's prodding, I decided it was time to apply for my own ministerial credentials. What a joy it was to be recognized at our last annual meeting standing beside our youngest son, who was receiving his own license to preach!

Now, of course, I'm writing this book. Even as I write the remaining pages, we're trusting God for whatever the next chapters in our lives may hold.

Lord, it's been an interesting ride. Thanks for staying in the boat. In Your wonderful name I pray. Amen.

Late humorist and author Erma Bombeck wrote, "Children need our love the most when they deserve it the least." We've always tried to assure our children that we love them, even if we don't love what they are doing. They don't always make it easy. Why? Perhaps they want to see if our love extends beyond the church and the many demands it makes on our time. But I believe it's something more. Truly acknowledging unconditional love requires a response. That means that they begin to feel the need to reconcile with those they've hurt, ultimately requiring that they make some lifestyle changes, something not all are willing to do until the consequences become harsh enough to force them to it.

That's why for some the road home is much longer than for others.

The same, of course, applies in a much greater sense to their relationship with God. Only He knows what it's going to take to bring them back to Him. And want to or not, friends, we're going along for the ride—up and down, round and round. And we'll meet a few satanically manufactured monsters along the way.

So what's a thrill ride hater like me to do? Stay in the boat and hold on tight. Know that many others are in the same boat. But God is, too. So no matter how long the ride, never give up hope.

Oh—and scream every now and then if you need to. I've been told it sometimes helps.

11

Will the Real Prodigal Please Stand Up?

Such were some of you.
—1 Cor. 6:11, NASB

It had been a lovely mother-daughter tea. Pastel tablecloths, baskets of spring flowers, and candles still adorned the tables, now scattered with crumbs and leftover bits of finger sandwiches, tea cakes, and scones. Ladies milled about, chatting and smiling, oblivious to the clink and clatter as volunteers in frilly aprons began clearing the china teapots and elegantly eclectic array of cups and saucers. It was apparent they were enjoying the extended fellowship.

Having been the speaker, I still stood near the front receiving those who had lingered to offer a greeting or express thanks. The chosen theme emphasizing the seasons of motherhood had prompted me at one point to allude briefly to the difficult years with my own children. Noticing more than a few misty eyes in the audience, I made it a special point to include mothers with prodigal children in my closing prayer. This prompted several to approach me afterward, sharing personal stories of both pain and praise.

Glancing to the side, I noticed a lovely young lady waiting patiently at the end of the rather lengthy line. Though dressed in faddish, youthful fashion, she was well groomed and had a fresh-scrubbed radiance. *She can't be a mom,* I thought. *Much too young.* When she finally stood before me, her words caught me off guard.

"Mrs. Braddy, I just had to tell you. I was your son."

Seeing my look of confusion, she proceeded. "For three years I was a prodigal, too. Living on the streets and doing drugs. I just, like, recently recommitted my life to the Lord. Don't ever stop praying for your son. God's gonna bring him back."

I was inexplicably touched. She had waited all this time just to share that encouragement. Voice hoarse with emotion, I thanked her. We chatted a few more minutes. Then she gave me a shy hug and turned to leave.

Still absorbing her words, I watched her walk away, arm in arm with her mom, who had also been waiting—a short and happy wait, no doubt, compared to the last three years. *Amazing,* I thought. *She looks like anything but a prodigal.*

But then what exactly does a prodigal look like?

People have a tendency to think of prodigals mostly as surly, rebellious children and often as sons (probably due in large part to the Bible story). But they come in all shapes, sizes, ages, and genders. How many might there be sitting in any given audience? My guess is that up to half the group could be comprised of past, present, or progressing prodigals. Still, you probably couldn't pick them out of a crowd of one.

Certainly some are more easily identified, those who in their altered state may have chosen to also permanently alter their appearance. But most bear no significant outward sign. Yet many still live with severe scars and continuing consequences. Truth is, we don't always know who they are or where they may be in the process. Only as God continues His work of grace in their lives are some able to face and find courage to relate the events of their past.

I received one such courageous confession from a former missionary's daughter, LeAnne Pyzer. It begins humbly, almost apologetically.

Dear Mrs. Braddy,

You probably don't remember me, but my mother says it was your women's group who sent us a much-needed Christmas care package while we were missionaries in Japan. I was only seven years old, not really rebel material.

Then LeAnne goes on to relate a story only those of us who have experienced the swift descent on the prodigal path could possibly understand. It started two missionary terms after the noted Christmas package. Following an enjoyable year in a stateside school, it was time once again for the family to return to the mission field. LeAnne, now age 16, didn't want to go. She began throwing fits, even threatening to run away from home. When that didn't work, she resorted to cursing, breaking curfew, and began hanging out with a questionable crowd.

"Maybe up to that point it was just typical teenage rebellion with a missionary kid twist," LeAnne reflects. What followed was anything but typical.

Hoping to make it impossible for her parents to return, she renounced God and began listening to heavy metal music and delving into witchcraft, Satanism, and other alternative religions. She also became sexually active. Within two months she was pregnant.

"I got the desired effect," admits LeAnne. "Mortified, my dad resigned missions and took a job as a Christian school superintendent." But by then their relationship was damaged to the point that after one particularly bad argument, LeAnne took her newborn and moved out. Her next mistake was a rapid rebound marriage followed by years of emotional and physical abuse, resulting in severe depression. Only after her husband deserted her did she and the children finally make their way back to her parents' home and an eventual recommitment of her life to the Lord.

"It was a long and painful journey," LeAnne is now able to admit, "but the Lord promised He would restore those lost years. And He has been faithful."

First God gave her a great job. Then, when least expected, He brought a wonderful and godly man into her life. They married, and he has since adopted her children.

Now the best part. She and her husband are currently pastoring alongside LeAnne's parents.

Praise the Lord! Not only is God still in the restoration business—He's an equal opportunity employer as well. That brings up another interesting point.

How many past prodigals do you suppose there are behind the pulpit? More than we might imagine. In his book *Good News About Prodigals,* Tom Bisset states that some research indicates that 93 percent of current pastors and Christian leaders had gone through a faith rejection that was either fairly or extremely serious but had come back stronger than ever.[1]

No doubt prodigals make some of the best pastors. When it comes to preaching the perils of the pigpen, they certainly know firsthand what they're talking about.

Maybe that's why my friend Philip Hicks enjoys having a pig as a pastoral sidekick. Through his ministry, Merry Heart Productions, Phil and his trained potbellied pig, Wilburt, delight, entertain, and share God's Word with any number of church, school, and civic events every year. Seeing Phil dressed in hillbilly attire and billing himself as Cousin Philburt, you would hardly guess that a little more than 20 years ago he was sentenced to life plus 15 years in prison for his participation in a drug money heist.

"Despite being 'trained up in the way I should go'," Phil states in his testimony tract, "I chose to rebel against my parents and society."[2]

By the late 70s he found himself associating with the rich and famous but also heavily involved in using and dealing in cocaine, leading to the incident for which he was sentenced.

But God had other plans.

Phil was also shot during that drug heist, a severe wound requiring a hospital stay of almost one year. Nineteen days into his treatment, he got a new overnight roommate—a young minister. During that 24-hour period, it just so happened that Phil was removed from heavy medication, and his guard was called to leave the room—just long enough for the providentially planted pastor to lead Phil back to the Lord.

That was only the first of many miracles that resulted in Phil being released only two years into his life sentence. Now, married with one child and two potbellied pigs, he and Wilburt travel, sharing his incredible testimony of God's love. Phil might be the only past prodigal who brought the pig home and put him to work.

Someone once said there are two categories of people: the righteous and the unrighteous—and usually it's the righteous who do the categorizing.

The first-century Corinthian church, the one most noted for preaching one thing while practicing another, probably thought they had a few prodigals pegged. If any folks knew a sinner when they saw one, it was First Church of Corinth. Trouble was, not only were they judging each other, they were also taking their troubles before secular judges. In the sixth chapter of his first letter to this church, Paul renders a rebuke and then proceeds to help them sort out their spiritual identity. In so doing, he makes a point of specifically listing those who won't enter heaven: idolaters, adulterers, thieves, drunkards, swindlers, just to name a few. I can just hear the self-righteous saints cheering him on. "Yeah, Paul—you tell 'em!"

Until he gets to the part recorded in verse 11.

"And that is what some of you were. But you were washed, you were sanctified, you were justified in the name of the Lord Jesus Christ and by the Spirit of our God" (emphasis added).

Oops.

What was Paul saying? Seems we are all prodigals until we embrace God's love and accept His plan of salvation. Even then some retain a remnant of the rebel, the bit that still at times demands their own selfish rights, often turning a deaf ear to the Heavenly Father's counsel. Yet God continues His progressive work of grace in all our lives.

I ask you—who needs to understand this more than those of us who have been called to minister that grace to others?

It has occurred to me more than once that maybe this is exactly why God allowed some of us to have prodigals of our very own, so we'll be forced to examine this propensity more closely, not only in our children but also in ourselves. Who, after all, can teach us more about compassion, the human condition, and God's amazing grace?

Chaplain Chuck Adams concurs: "My experience with a prodigal child," he says, "has taught me far more about forgiveness and grace than I ever learned in seminary."

Hopefully we've also learned a bit about judgment. Some of us know firsthand the pain of watching our children harden their appearance, mark their bodies, and lose their innocence. No question that they do it on purpose just to get a reaction. How many times have we been witnesses to that reaction in the staring eyes of those not quick enough to hide the disdain? It hurts to know what they must be thinking of our child—and us.

Does it give us a glimpse of how those in the world must feel when (if) they decide to give the church one more try, only to get that same reaction? Paul is right. The people he described in 1 Corinthians aren't going to enter heaven—especially when some aren't too sure they want them to enter the church either.

The last time we visited our oldest son, we took him to church, one we were in hopes he might like and begin attending. We were sadly disappointed. It was soon apparent that everything in the service was geared toward believers. Fact is, anyone attending who had not been raised in church would have had no clue what was going on. Seeker sensitive? How about prodigal perceptive?

Admittedly we're all guilty of making snap judgments.

We met Karissa when she and our oldest son began spending time together after he moved to Idaho. My son assured me it wasn't a romantic relationship, but that didn't keep me from fearing the worst.

"Don't worry, Mom," he told me. If only I had a dollar for every time I've heard that. "Actually, I think you'll like Karissa."

The next summer we finally got acquainted. Karissa has lovely red hair, big blue eyes, weighs 90 pounds soaking wet, and is sweet as anything. So what if she has a few tasteful tattoos? My son was right. I liked her. That was even before I discovered she's a committed Christian with a couple of missionary outreaches under her tiny belt. I was grateful God had brought someone into our son's life with a positive influence.

When Karissa recently left Idaho with plans to attend a design school near us, we happily invited her to stay here. Her car—the one with the bumper sticker that reads *Jesus Loves Me With or Without My Tatoos*—now adorns our driveway.

If there's any portion of Scripture we with prodigals have committed to memory, it's the Luke 15 passage. Besides its faith-inspiring finale, it reminds us there's more than one reason a person becomes a prodigal.

Some, like the sheep, are lost by accident. Perhaps they are those who have somehow lost their sense of direction and then wandered until they went too far and got caught in a terrible tangle.

There might also be those who have suffered some form of collateral damage as discussed in an earlier chapter. Either way, they need someone to seek and find them, untangle them, lovingly bind their wounds, and then treat them with care and compassion all the way home.

Then there are those like the coin, lost by neglect. While someone wasn't paying attention, they slipped away. Sometimes all it takes is to sweep away the dirt and hurt in order to find the person of value beneath.

Cheryl was a teenager in one of our first youth groups, the

youngest daughter in a large family of lovely and talented siblings. I'll never forget her words when, a few years later, she came to thank us for being part of her life. "You're the first youth pastors who ever called me by my first name." Before that she had been known only as one of the Hutson girls.

It could be that we, too, must rid ourselves of unnecessary clutter in order to more clearly see those around us who are neglected and lost.

The portion of Luke 15 with which we're most familiar is that of the lost son, the child lost by his own choice. With rebellious resolution, he has sped out of sight, though never out of heart. Seemingly there is little those who love these fugitives can do but wait until circumstances force them home. That doesn't mean God won't provide others to help them along the journey.

There's one more reason we must never stop praying and watching.

Aren't you thankful that though God shut Eden's gates, He didn't lock heaven's door? He, too, watches from the portals for those coming up the path. Here's how Phil Milton, a past prodigal, expresses his gratitude to the God who pursues: "I'm thankful to God because, contrary to the old adage, God helps those who cannot help themselves. He exists to make the blind see and the deaf hear, to free the captives and speak good news. He does not stand back and wait for those well enough to approach him but pursues those who are sick, even (and especially) by their own doing. He is the great chaser. And though sometimes we are equally great at playing hard to get, He lives to win us over."

Now we come to a favorite phrase in the prodigal parable. *So he got up and went to his father. But while he was still a long way off, his father saw him* (Luke 15:20).

If there's one thing we must help every prodigal understand, it's that from any far-flung destination, it's only one step back to God. And the minute prodigals come within sight of home—we'll be running out to meet them.

Yes, there are prodigals all around us, in all stages of the return journey. We're not the only parents who are waiting and watching. But we're also pastors. Even as we scan the outlying landscape for our own, we must not lose sight of the need to help others. Every homecoming can be a vicarious victory.

Then it's party time.

Though the young minister God planted in Phil Hicks' hospital room had only an initial 24-hour assignment, it wasn't the last Phil saw of him. The next day he and members from his church came back with presents and a cake to celebrate Phil's first full day as a Christian. They were joined, according to Luke, by an unseen angelic assembly.

I suppose they could have let the angels celebrate alone. But they wanted to be sure Phil heard the happiness. Perhaps Gladys Bronwyn Stern said it best: "Silent gratitude isn't much use to anyone." Every time a sinner surrenders, we should whoop it up—and share the joy by putting those who have prayed and encouraged over the years on the invitation list.

Then keep loving them. Here's one final testimony from my friend Judy Phillips, a licensed minister and educator: "Our prodigal daughter (who was only 15 when she had their now-23-year-old grandson) said it helped her a lot in her decision to return, because we still loved her when she was out there in the world. She could sense God's love even when she was away from Him. Today she is very, very strong in the Lord."

Here Judy sums it up for us: "It's hard to believe her past considering who she is now."

What does a prodigal look like? A person in need of God's grace.

And such were all of us.

Lord, how we all stand in need of Your grace and mercy! Let us grasp once again how generously and freely You give it. Then help us offer it in the same way to others. Assure us that even as You bring those who need Your love across our paths, You are placing others in the path of our own prodigal for the same purpose. In Jesus' beautiful name we pray. Amen.

I suppose we might all be put off a little if we came across a prodigal in the guise of a declared Communist and atheist. A number of years ago my husband and I were invited to the central European country of Slovakia as Christian camp speakers. There we met Anna. Seventeen years old at the time, she spoke fluent English and served as our interpreter. In our short time together, we developed a strong bond and have kept in touch over the years.

We soon learned of Anna's concern for her grandfather, who

despite the family's Christian background, had declared himself a Communist and an atheist for more than 60 years. When Anna wrote me recently of her grandfather's conversion to Christ, I knew it needed to be placed in this book as an encouragement—first, that we should never stop praying and speaking words of love and encouragement into our prodigals' lives; second, that as long as a prodigal is alive, it's never too late to make his or her way home.

Over ten years ago, before he came to Christ, Anna's grandfather began having heart problems, which eventually precipitated two strokes. He recovered but continued in the care of doctors and medicine. It was during his last hospitalization a year ago that the pastor and an elder from the family's church came to visit. Here, through Anna's interpretation, are her grandfather's own charming words describing the amazing change:

"It is good to have lots of friends and acquaintances around you. Two of my good friends visited me (in the hospital) and offered to pray. They also taught me how to ask Jesus for help. These friends have helped me to find a new journey to life. I am very grateful to them.

"After we prayed together, I have asked Jesus Christ to forgive my sins and take me under His care. Since then, I have read many good materials that helped me think about spiritual things and understand what I did not know before. I often pray to God, and although I still suffer from my illness, I feel relief."

What a relief for us as well, to be reminded that God has a plan for Communists and con artists, for preachers and prodigals—and the process in between! My prayer is that it may rekindle in us such a compassionate caring and love for the lost that, even as our arms reach out to encompass our own precious prodigals, their circle might be expanded to encompass the world's wandering weary.

As we face the challenge, there's no doubt we'll find ourselves caught at times between the rock in our own hearts and the pinnacle where God wants to place us—a perch providing eternal perspective.

12

Between a Rock and a God Place

I lift up my eyes to the hills—where does my help come from? My help comes from the LORD, the Maker of heaven and earth.
—Ps. 121:1-2

Fall has come once again—another season of change and reflection.

It was five years ago when Jim's office relocated, bringing us back to Sacramento and full circle in many ways. Twenty seasons have passed now since we first moved here. Hard to believe.

Recently I found myself driving back through the old neighborhood. I hadn't really planned to, but with time to spare between appointments in the area and this book unfolding in my heart, I felt drawn. Somehow I needed to feel for myself the changes these seasons have brought, not necessarily just to the neighborhood.

Pulling around the corner, I stopped the car in front of a small park near our old house. Unlike that long-ago autumn, climate conditions this year had resulted in just a few yellow tinges. Only the cooler air, producing a dust-and-dry-leaf scent, gave indication that change is coming.

From my parking place I could see all the way to the end of the street—the same one Jim and I walked, weighing his decision to resign the church. The houses and landscape had changed little. *How is that possible,* I wondered, *when everything else has changed so much?*

As I watched, a few leaves detached themselves and fluttered in slow circles to the ground. My mind circled back as well.

Only a month before, we had visited our oldest son and the grandchildren in Idaho. We had a good time and some good talks.

Outwardly there were some encouraging changes. But inwardly we sensed the same old struggle. For reasons known only to God, he just can't seem to let go of some of the old hurts and habits. Is it still the fear of failure? Or has that merely become a convenient excuse? Whatever, the result is the same: sadness and a still-simmering anger. Granted, it's more controlled now, no longer directed at us. But unfortunate recent incidents have proven it still doesn't take much to make it boil over.

On our last day there we stood saying good-bye—again. My arms barely reached around my son's husky shoulders. Stepping back, I looked into his face. He looked tired.

Why don't you just come home? I wanted to say. It's easy to think that maybe in a different setting, things would be different.

But it wasn't going to happen. Hadn't we just talked about it the day before?

"Ever think about moving closer?" I had asked.

"It would be nice," he spoke wistfully, then looked down at his small son. "But this is where I live now, Mom."

I understood. Yet I couldn't help feeling that in a symbolic sense, it also spoke of where he is living spiritually.

"Well. Find a dentist and get that tooth fixed. We'll pay for it." I had to fix something. I'm his mother.

As for the rest, we would simply have to continue trusting God. With the old rock weighing heavy in my heart, I could only pray once more, *Don't let it be long, Lord, until he finally surrenders.*

Then I remember a sudden shower of leaves bringing me back to the place where the pain began.

Truth is, 20 seasons later, it no longer matters what created our sons' problems. We're way beyond that. It has come down to this: our children will always be the most important things in the world to us. Of all our earthly possessions, they're the only things we can take to heaven with us. With all the faith that's in us, we continue to believe that we will. The only thing that matters now is the outcome. For that, our hope rests in God.

Still, the process in between has to count for something. There's no question as to how much God has already been at work in all our lives. Looking back, we see that it's the only way any of us could have survived. The parts of our story that I selected for this book can't begin to describe the conflagration of conflicting emotions over all the years—hurt and pain that were often intermingled with hope and happiness.

Long ago we began to understand that our problems could not be relegated only to our prodigal. God was using the circumstances of our lives to work in all of us. I believe it was invaluable that we, as pastors, reached the point of no longer seeing imperfection as failure—rather to see that to be imperfect is to be human, and that by recognizing that humanness we admit our great need for God.

It has kept us real before God and humble in our own sight. One writer summed it up this way: "I've found that facing some of these shame-filled problems tenderizes us and helps to make us real."

Ever notice how personal experience can cause scripture to jump off the page? Take for instance the passage in Rom. 5:3-5. "We also rejoice in our sufferings, because we know that suffering produces perseverance; perseverance, character; and character, hope. And hope does not disappoint us, because God has poured out his love into our hearts by the Holy Spirit, whom he has given us."

Here's what my life lessons have taught me: seems you can't get character without perseverance. Character means discovering who we are—or more accurately who God expects us to be—then beginning to act accordingly. In order to do that, we must strive to understand who God is and what He expects. Once we know God, we can't help but see His great heart of love. Because He loves us, we have hope. In turn, hope inspires us with a greater determination to persevere. Like the seasons, it's a cycle that repeats itself, orchestrated by the Holy Spirit.

Once I understood these things, I had to humbly acknowledge the great chasm sin places between God and us and how He daily and faithfully fills it with His love and mercy. Yes, Jeremiah—His compassions are new every morning. How, then, can we not extend the same compassion to others? What an impact this has made on our ministry!

Because we've persevered, we're stronger in our faith and better in our relationships. How else can it be explained that despite our defenses and differences—even our children's refusal to openly embrace faith—we're closer as a family because of what we've tackled together? The saying comes to mind, "That which doesn't kill us makes us strong."

All this has given us faith to know that the eventual outcome will be God's doing, not our own. He will get the ultimate glory. And that's as it should be.

Through it all, we've done our best to follow God's leading and fulfill His call on our lives to minister to others, to be faithful and personally responsible, even when our children weren't. How thankful I am that my husband's compulsion to resign 20 years ago didn't take!

No doubt we all know by now that staying the course requires an unshakeable determination.

Growing up in the Midwest, Jim and I both remember with some chagrin the old-fashioned testimony times in church. Though meant to be an encouragement, inevitably some dear saint would end up sharing a long litany of laments, then conclude by saying, "Just pray for me that I hold out to the end." Both of us purposed early on to make our lives count for a bit more than just holding out. Maybe in that way it *was* an encouragement.

Still, when I prayed, *Lord, let my life make a difference,* I had no idea what I was in for. But then if I had, would I have prayed it?

Tom Peters said, "Unless you walk out into the unknown, the odds of making a profound difference in your life are pretty low."

No doubt there are minutes on the ministry circuit when all of us would like to either give up or go up. But instead, God is asking us to go on. It's those days when we find ourselves living "between a rock and a hard place." We must determine over and over how we're going to live with the consequences of choices our children or others make. We must try to look up when circumstances are weighing us down and live someplace between the hurt and the hope.

Yet we know that with God's help all things are possible. It's as we trust Him and keep putting one foot in front of the other that we find ourselves, instead, between a rock and a "God place."

Of course, we all have our own pet rocks. The day I laid down a big one was the day I realized that I had to forgive my children even before they asked for it. Only then was I able to begin to love them unconditionally with no strings or promises of good behavior attached. What a weight that lifted!

Some of us continue to carry the rocks only because we don't know where to drop them.

A few years ago I attended a women's conference in which author Jill Briscoe was the speaker. I was surprised but encouraged to hear her tell the story of walking through the pain of her daughter's devastating divorce. She poignantly described her pain, the times of questioning God, and the many tears she shed. She finally came to realize that though she couldn't do anything to reverse what had happened, God wanted to use her to speak into the lives of her grandchildren. That meant that she needed to stop grieving and start redirecting her energies. Her advice was this: "Don't waste the tears."

Perhaps there are some of us who are still hurt and angry over what has transpired in our children's lives. Take Jill's advice, and direct that anger at the devil. Then begin to seek God for divine redirection. That's when we begin to see the promising possibilities of how He'll use the pain for our growth and His glory. Simply put, we must allow the pain, disappointment, and frustration to make us better, not bitter.

Perhaps the most touching tribute to God's grace I ever witnessed was at yet another Mother's Day tea where I spoke. At a table in front of the speaker's podium sat two women. One was obviously older, though the other bore some recognizable signs of premature aging associated with substance abuse. The younger woman seemed to be in distress, crying and often bent over as if in pain. The older lady was doing her best to comfort her.

What I found out later was that the older lady's son had recently died of a drug overdose. The woman in distress was his girlfriend. His mother had brought the strung-out girlfriend to this lovely tea in an attempt to show love and reach her for Christ.

That precious mom was in a place that none of us ever want to be. Yet somehow she was able to rise above the rubble and put herself in a "God place."

For many of us with prodigals, the last chapter of our journey has yet to be written. The words will be the events in our lives and the lives of our children. Scripture tells us that God is the Author and the Finisher of our faith. How long before He's finished? Only He knows.

So with a good dose of heavenly patience and spirit-given hope, we wait.

Here's a little thought to nibble on while you're waiting. It was my husband who reminded me of something easily missed in the biblical account of the prodigal son. However long it took for the biblical prodigal to come to his senses, the father kept a robe and ring waiting. He never gave up hope.

He was just waiting for the day when he could throw a party, get out the robe and ring—and rejoice.

For those of you whose prodigals have come home, we celebrate with you!

For those whose prodigals may be only a speck on the horizon, we're lacing up our tennis shoes for the sprint.

For those who still wait, we commit ourselves to watching and praying together.

Just keep the robe and ring dusted.

I can't think of a more pastoral way to close than to offer you a scripture and a prayer. 2 Tim. 1:12 is one of my life verses and a perfect fit for those in every stage of the prodigal journey.

I am not ashamed, because I know whom I have believed, and am convinced that he is able to guard what I have entrusted to him for that day.

Let's pray it as a promise.

Lord, we know Your nature. It is to love, to seek, and to save. It is not Your will that any should perish. There's no question about it. We're determined to trust You—to know Your power and understand Your unlimited ability. Nothing is too hard for You.

Lord, we're depending on You to keep our prodigals safe every step of the way back home. We've fully entrusted our children to You, because You're fully trustworthy. Believing You know what's best, we'll accept Your timing.

Now, Lord, because we trust You, we ask that You use whatever circumstances You see fit to bring our children home. In the meantime, give us peace and patience, wisdom and direction. May Your Word and Holy Spirit provide comfort in the waiting, company in the vigil, and hope for the coming celebration.

And everybody said . . .

Amen.

Notes

Chapter 2
1. Cynthia Hubert, "Grief's Emotions Can Also Have Physical Effect," *Sacramento Bee,* September 3, 2003.

Chapter 3
1. Taken from <www.bobssermons.com>. Tom Bisset, *Good News About Prodigals* (Grand Rapids: Discovery House, 1997).

Chapter 6
1. Milton Lee, "Pastoring with Hurts at Home" (*Leadership Magazine,* 1989), 98-105.

Chapter 8
1. Tom Mullen, *Seriously, Life Is a Laughing Matter* (Nashville: Word Publishing, 1981), 19.
2. Barbara Johnson, *Highlights from "So Stick A Geranium In Your Hat and Be Happy"* (Nashville: Word Publishing, 1993), 62.

Chapter 11
1. Taken from <www.bobssermons.com>. Tom Bisset, *Good News About Prodigals* (Grand Rapids: Discovery House, 1997).
2. Read Phil Hicks' entire testimony on his Web site: <www.amerryheart.com>.